Definitely Maybe, Probε

Definitely Maybe, Probably Not.

Fae Glesga Tae Goa.

James Joseph Toner

BOGANY PRESS
GLASGOW

A WEE INDEPENDENT PUBLISHING HOOSE

contact@jamesjtoner.co.uk

Edited by Iain Donnelly @ Saraswati Publishing, Cambodia.

Acknowledgements

I have too many people to thank to mention them all by name but I appreciate all the support given to me during the Indian jail part of my experience, especially Big Mick, Wee Tosh, Steevo, Willie S, Ed, Pete, Asa, Moonz, Tam and John, Ryan, Strain, Gal, wee Jeff and anyone else I might not be aware of who contributed to my bail when it became a possibility or who sent money over to help me out during the experience. I'll never forget that.

Mick and Tosh for making survival inside and while on bail possible.

The McGurins, Ed and Carol, for the contribution they made to the fighting fund. Thanks for that. Too many tae mention. Anne Kerr and wee Izzy, you know what for. McDowall as well.

To Mick Farrell for all his efforts with my Facebook and the graphics he's worked tirelessly on for me. He's made this cover and much more besides possible. Gordon Waddell for the original photo that turned into the painting of my old house in Bogany Terrace, which was painted by the very talented Leanne Dawson.

Wee Rab fae Govan for being Wee Rab fae Govan.

To Iain Donnelly, my editor, for pulling all this together and turning it into a book. No mean feat that.

If I've forgotten anyone, it's not deliberate, just a sign that this old memory disnae work as well as it used tae. So if your name's not on that list but you have been part of my journey, then thank you to you too. And thanks also to everyone who contributed to the crowdfunder. You guys made this possible. Last but by no means least, a big massive thank you tae ma Mum, wee Agnes. For everything she has ever did and still continues to do for me. Love ye Ma xx

Martin, this book is for you.

Introduction

In many ways, the story you are about to read is just the story of an ordinary bloke, albeit an ordinary bloke who had some extraordinary experiences. I had no real plans to write these experiences down, but so many people have told me I need to, and so many others have said there are lessons to be learned from my experiences, that I have bowed to the pressure.

I grew up in a normal environment, so I want to emphasise now that in no way am I blaming anyone around me, or indeed the places I lived, for how things turned out (or how I turned out either). I'm not proud of everything I did, but nor am I ashamed either. And I'm not bigging myself up in any way, I'm just telling the story the way it happened.

I went to school then I left school. I started drinking then moved onto drugs, pretty much the standard for anyone my age growing up on a council estate – or schemes as we call them in Scotland. I drank more, I took more drugs, and then one day, inevitably, the wheels came off the bus. But through it all, I remained a decent bloke (a good friend told me I had to include that point). I started selling small amounts of drugs then moved up the ladder and was moving quite a lot of them. Again, I'm not bragging or seeking absolution, it's just the way things were.

There were times I was a wee toe rag, and there were times I was a lousy drug dealer and gave away or used more than I actually sold. But there came a day when I walked away from it all and got myself a normal job with normal people. I don't use the word 'normal' to offend anyone; it's just a reflection of society's perceptions so easier to use those terms.

My story covers several major events which affected me deeply. The first of those was my brother's murder and how I dealt – or didn't deal – with it. I believe that other people cannot break you – you can only allow them to break you, and I think that was a mistake I made often. Life is a long learning process, and I know I am still learning even as I write this down. So the first part of my story is about me growing up, my early life experiences, and the events surrounding my brother's murder. It then deals with my extended tip to Goa in India, the debacle of my arrest and imprisonment on remand, and ends with me being granted bail.

The second book will deal with my trial and experiences of the excruciatingly slow Indian justice process, the lows of almost losing hope, the highs of the support I received from friends and family, and the relief and emotion of finally returning home to my loved ones and to Glasgow. It also deals with the trial that took place regarding my brother's murder.

The third book – which I am starting work on very soon – will deal with journeys of a different type. With everything that happened in my life, there have been times when it is hard to keep it real/unreal (delete as appropriate). I discovered a lot about life, and even more about myself. I got into – and read a lot about - Buddhism, Eckhart Tolle, Chaos Magick, Meditation, which helped me build and develop coping mechanisms that have helped immensely. I learned to be patient, but still find it hard to attain sometimes. I learned anger management strategies, but again occasionally find it hard to do too. I began to believe that all living things are part of the universe, and that all living things are connected through a collective or universal stream of consciousness. I still contradict myself a lot as you will tell in a moment or two. But through the three parts of this book I believe I have changed and grown, and without that growth and change I may not be here today to tell the story.

So I`ve been bad, turned good, got a bad break and sort of went bad again. Had a few shit years then came to India where I found myself like George Harrison had before me. Loads of people have, but I thought it would be cool to slide his name into my book; don't know many famous people so I just dropped his name in there - Jai Guru Deva Aum George. He managed to live a spiritual life in our shitey material world.

A friend once told me that a book is a series of reflections and that's exactly what I am trying to write here; the reflections on my life so far. A life that has taken me to hell and back. That may sound quite melodramatic but you will realise it is pretty close to the truth.

I keep saying I am not a writer, but someone wise (my editor) told me I'm a great storyteller, and that is sometimes more important than technical writing skills, so I'll take his word for it. I am not very disciplined in my writing and I change my mind on a regular basis, so this book has been written over the space of almost two years to date. The problem with that, if you believe it to be a problem, is I may appear to regularly contradict myself. The reason for that is that through this journey I want to take you on, my belief patterns have been constantly changing and because of this I am a regular contradictor. So if you want to take the time to spot my contradictions, fire in, but please don't let it distract from the story itself.

I like to tell myself that there is something for everyone in my story, but I can't see Theresa fuckin May, Boris, or our even our very own First Minister, Mrs. Sturgeon being remotely interested; they have far much bigger fish to fly (correct spelling). I`ll move on and continue with the "yarn" as one budding yarner once called it. I`m guilty of making up my own words as well, which in telling you that I hope it saves any of the Contra/Spelling Police their own time in which they can go and do their checking elsewhere.

I have done many jobs in my almost 48 years, and I will cover some if not all of them in the pages that follow. I am just a bloke with time on his hands who wants to tell his story, we all have one remember so never be afraid to tell yours. I am honest in the words I am writing, and not very proud of some of the deeds I have carried out during my past. But the past is where they are now so I don't stare at them anymore. Have a wee look now and again maybe, but no need to stare at them.

If I have any regrets, it's the life I have taken off my mother and the start I haven't given to my son. A mother's love is unconditional and she forgives me and all my wrong doings. Rebuilding a relationship with my fifteen-year-old son may prove a little bit more difficult. He would have heard stories about his dad and the madness that surrounded me, but we don't always believe what we hear. We do though believe what we see. I hope one day he is proud that his dad has come through some crazy shit and came out that softer gentler person. I also hope that one day he will consider me his friend.

I was travelling on the train to the capital of India, New Delhi when I received a text message telling me of a bomb blast in the city. 14 people had lost their lives at the time of me writing this introduction to my story. A story of my life and the various life situations I found myself experiencing during it.

The news of the blast made me think back to a time when I had suffered a loss in my life, and I thought about the families of the unfortunates who had been caught up in the explosion. I wondered for a minute how the families and the loved ones left behind would be feeling at that time and how they would deal with the loss that had been dealt to them.

When my own family had suffered the loss of my younger brother back in 2004 I hadn't dealt with it too well. I allowed myself to drift into a depression that I now know could have been avoided. I suppose it`s quite easy to say that with hindsight, but I didn't know then what I know today about myself, especially in relation to the world I live in. I knew about spirituality from my time in a 12-step programme, but I could not put into practice what I had learned in that time. It is only in the past three years or so that I have managed to get a real handle on it and it's that which had made my present life situation much easier to cope with.

I will attempt to describe to you the life I lived and how I have felt during the various stages of that life. From a young boy who grew up with no father to the man I have become this day. From someone who always wanted to be someone else to the person who is happy within himself and with being James Toner. From someone who would have done almost anything to get money to have the material things that today I realise are not as important to me in my current situation. Of course in writing this I realise we all need those bits of paper, tokens, and in the years to come the plastic invisible thing that will replace all of the above. At this stage I don't want to get all political on you but there is a New World Order on its way and what better way to track and trace people than through the purchases they make and where they make them.

I had to begin by discarding all that I had grown to believe to be the truth. By changing all the thoughts that I had grown to accept because of my conditioning during the earlier stages of my life and begin again from scratch. We allow the mind to control our thoughts, feelings and actions. That need not be the case. We can control the mind instead of the other way about. And it's not even difficult to achieve, smiling to myself as I write that because I am yet to master that as well.

So that`s how I found myself almost 3000 metres high in the Himalayas attempting to write my story. If you're reading this, I thank you for taking the time to do so. If you actually paid hard earned paper cash for it, I am forever in your debt.

For me, my aim is to put my thoughts into words and on to paper and for those words to carry some sort of meaning. I think I have revisited words that have held me back during my life. Fear, worry, yesterday, words that mean nothing to me today. Today I have learned to live in the present moment and not think about the past or indeed the future too much if even at all.

As I have already stated, the life I lived and the life situations that I continue to find myself in are slightly different from most other people's. I feel that it is my duty, if you like, to let people know how I coped with situations that were not normal to me, and if one person takes anything from my ramblings then my life's ambition to write a book will have been worthwhile. Everybody wants to write a book, don't they? We all have a story to tell so why not write that book.

If you take anything away from this book, then I hope it is that you can see that we can make this life easier by living life each day at as it comes, putting our past firmly behind us, and not for a single second should we worry about the future. The modern day spiritual teacher, Eckhart Tolle, would laugh at this point and reminds us that the future is yet to happen and we are in fact worrying about something that does not exist. I`d call that almost akin to madness, but as my writing progresses I may even contradict Mr. Tolle himself...

So once again I thank you if you are taking the time to read this story, and please think what you like about the guy who has written it.

My name is James...and this is my story.

PART ONE

Chapter 1: The Early Years

My past, what a load of shite in my opinion. Aye I know, some of you are sitting there thinking: "This guy tells us he's going to write about his past then tells us it's a load of shite?" Well I did warn you there would be contradictions. But to tell my story, I need to include my past. It's necessary to include it as it is part of my journey, the departure point if you will, and without it, I wouldn't have made that journey or be where I am now. At this point, I could be a right smart arse and reel off the following quote and author as if it had sprung from some fount of internal wisdom, but the truth is I only half remembered it and had to get onto Google to get the wording and the source right too.

"The past is a foreign country; they do things differently there." — L.P. Hartley, The Go-Between

That sort of nails it for me, we all think of the past in different ways, but I try not to dwell too much on it. I, like everyone I know, have fantastic memories of the past, but I try to forget the hang-ups which start the wee games going in our minds and allows our EGO to take control again. Now if you don't know what I mean by EGO, I'm not a psychologist so my explanation would probably be way off. As I will probably be doing at various points throughout the book, I will point you in the direction of Google to get a better definition than I could supply. If you find yourself reading about Sigmund Freud's structural model of the psyche, then you're headed in the right direction.

One of the good things about writing an autobiography in this day and age is that most of it can be evidenced on the internet. The names I will mention and the accusations made against them have not come from me. It`s all out there for the world to read and watch but the British Government have totally ignored my pleas, and in fact forty-six months after my arrest they have not even allowed me to speak to anyone British. I will attempt to cover that later in my "yarn". I am being flippant in the use of the word yarn of course, what I am writing is a touch more than a yarn I`d say.

Like I have already said, I was this normal wee boy from Glasgow who one day found himself living in South Africa because the economic climate in the UK at the time was pretty bad. Cards from school friends, lots of goodbyes, the Catholic Church even brought forward my first holy communion for me so I could take the body of Christ before my parents began their new life in South Africa. My tongue is firmly planted in my cheek as I write that, the body of Christ...

In the UK, workers were forced by the Conservative government to work 3 days per week instead of the 5 that was the norm, and my father being a plumber saw the opportunity to move away to better the lives of his family. I have often wondered why South Africa; it was in the early 1970s and at the height of apartheid and I don't believe my father was a racist in any way shape or form. My mum doesn't really speak of it, but I take it that South Africa would have just been the better financial option at the time.

Although still in my pre-teens, I knew that something wasn't right in the country. Black people used separate buses, lived in separate housing, and at nine each evening a siren sounded giving the indigenous population one hour to get back to their townships or face consequences of which I was unaware. Of course, I am now aware what was going on in that hellhole of a country, most likely the exact same as what's going on there just now, only the worm has turned and the majority black population, who are still the poorest, will be getting years of their own back. I can say that with fact because I still have family who live there in a compound surrounded by a six-foot barbed wired fence patrolled by killer dogs into the bargain. What we saw in the 2010 Football World Cup is not the real South Africa. Anyway...

School life was great in South Africa, and I would perhaps have been prop forward for the Springboks had we stayed there into my later years. For any non-rugby fan the Prop is the guy who holds up about 200 kilos of muscle in the scrum. We played cricket and had lessons outside in the sunshine. My father ran an amateur football team, and much of the weekend was spent watching the game being played out there. There was a fair sized international community, so I reckon the level of football would have been not too bad. Still no black players to be seen though, no black referees either, but I didn't give it much thought. To be honest, we were told to stay away from "them" and that's exactly what we did. A few years after our return, my cousin came back for a holiday and I asked him about the black people. This was a long time ago but his words were pretty close to this: "The Kafir; he is alright as long as he behaves himself." I don't think I need to continue with that part of the tale.

Life in South Africa was great until one day I got out of my bed and found my father dying on the bathroom floor. My mother was bent over the top of him crying when I got out of my bed for school that morning. I was sent along to a neighbour's house to call an ambulance, and she also called my dad's sister Jannette. Aunt Jannette and her husband Andy arrived and took me and Martin away to their house which wasn't far from our wee flat. That was the Friday morning and I can't really remember feeling anything about it if I`m honest. I played with my cousins and had fun as I always had at their house. Big garden and lots to do, that's what I recall of that day. On the Saturday evening, there was a phone call to the house which my uncle Andy answered, I remember that as clear as day. After that much wailing from the living room until Andy came into tell us my dad was dead.

He was 34 years old and had died of a brain haemorrhage. Just like that, no warning. Apparently, according to my mother, we were back in Scotland within 2 weeks and that was that. No other man ever entered my life in the shape of a father figure. No one ever explained what the fuck had happened to my dad. 'God needed plumbers in heaven' we were told and that was that. No one told this 10-year-old what was expected of him, so I grew up a confused wee guy who was continually told he was the man of the house and who had to fill his father's shoes. In that lies the root of all my future life hang-ups.

Was I fuck, I was ten years old and had lost my da overnight, and in those days there was no one who ever sat the young person down and explained death to them. All I continually remember is being told that I was the man of the house and should be acting in the proper manner. Never mind I had school or anything like that. I know now I grew up with a chip on my shoulder but I don't blame anyone for that, that is the way it was in those days and that's the way it was going to be with me. In the 1970s death was still a taboo subject in terms of talking about it to young people and I was no different

We returned from South Africa and I went back to school in Glasgow, Castlemilk to be exact. Castlemilk was a sprawling estate that had been built in the 1950s to contain the overspill from the slum buildings that were being knocked down in the Gorbals and Bridgeton at the time. Big masses of houses and latterly multi-storey blocks of flats. Fantastic accommodation for the folk who had been living ten or more to a house with a room and kitchen, but with not one single amenity. There was fuck all in it for people to take their minds off work and life. Not even a fucking pub until the 1980s. Castlemilk was like one of the American projects, and I was to become one of the street players but not for a couple of years yet.

Anyhow I'm not here to write about Castlemilk, plenty of good and bad stuff has been written about the area already, and can be found in the local library or the internet.

I`m here to tell you about me growing up, or I should just say getting older I suppose.

I went to school and was a fairly average pupil who with a bit of direction and prompting could perhaps have made something of his life academically, but I know that wasn't to be the road for me. I was popular at school with everyone, never bullied, and had the ability to make even the hardest and rottenest lads laugh. I was wee Jim Toner at the time and school was ok, I went when I wanted to and left with 5 O Grades. Average I suppose.

I came from a family of plumbers and it was in the building game that I was to find my first job. Working under one of Margaret Thatcher's schemes, The Y.O.P or Youth Opportunity Program to give it its proper title. What a lot of shite that name was for a start, because we may have been youth, but we got no fuckin opportunity from the £23 per week that the job paid and were merely used to bring down the unemployment figures that had peaked at 1 in 10. People in the UK had no work at that time in 1981/82.

My first job was with a firm called Tropic Heating and Plumbing, and I was on a promise that at the end of the 6 month course I would be made up to apprentice status. Looking back at the figure of 23 pounds per week, perhaps that was all I was due to get considering the significance of the number in my later years. I`ll try and explain later.

Anyway, as is the way of these things, I didn`t get the promised job and once my 6 months were over I was shown the door by my father's friend. I don't blame him because I can now understand how bad things actually were at the time. Margaret Thatcher killed the industries in Scotland and the working class parts of England and Wales during her tenure. That again is just one of the many opinions of this writer.

I did what I had to do and went and found work for myself, on my own, and without the help of anyone in the family of plumbers. I say family of plumbers, but it was my dad and his young brother Frank who plumbed. I stayed in the trade incidentally, but I was never going to be any good at plumbing and that's a fact.

While I say I didn't get any help, I did use the name of my Uncle Frank, my dad`s brother, to get me in the door of the firm he worked with. In later years I let Frank down badly and that is one if the first things I intend to sort out when I get back to Scotland. It wasn`t work related but it is one of the few major regrets I have in my life. He is a good man, and his wife, my aunt Agnes, is a lovely lady and I took advantage of their kind nature. Junkies do it all the time, and at the time I'll talk about later I was just that. A fucked up junkie, no more or less, was all I was at that time. During my time here my Aunt Agnes has left this life and I will never be able to make amends for the wrong I did to her.

So I strolled into the offices of Davie Campbell & Son one Monday morning and told them I had heard that they may be taking on plumbers.

"Do you know anyone who works here?" I was asked.

"Yes, Frank Toner is my uncle but he doesn't know I'm down here looking for work".

"What do you know about plumbing?" This guy asked me.

I told him I had just completed my YOP in plumbing, and he asked me a few questions that I answered ok I suppose because he offered me the job.

"When can you start?"

"Tomorrow morning." I replied.

And that was how I became one of the worst plumbers ever to grace God's earth, me and my mate Gary, but we were never made to be plumbers. He was a top shagger and I was destined to almost 20 years of problematic drinking, addiction, and crime. It was to be a few years before I entered the lower divisions of the shagging league, but I suppose I did work my way up through the divisions and only suffered relegation on occasion.

I hated being a plumber from the start, but it paid not bad money, and it was during my second year of my apprenticeship that I was introduced to drugs for the first time. By drugs I don't mean alcohol, although I now believe alcohol to be the worst drug on the market, one that is readily available from pubs, clubs, and shops, and can even be delivered to your door. All taxed by the government of course, and it has become revenue they cannot do without. I had already discovered that beast and it had its claws into me from the start.

The very first time I got drunk, I was sick and was crying for my dad who had been dead for around 4/5 years at this point. I was about 15 years old, and in Malta on holiday with my auntie Margaret - my mum's sister - her husband Robert, and their daughter Lillian. We had attended a BBQ and at first a couple of glasses of wine were dished out. I became the "funniest guy in the place", or so I would have imagined I'm sure. Then I tried to take over the mic from the guy who was playing musical chairs. Everyone thought this was hilarious, so the latent alcoholic in me played on this and I got worse. The sickness and the abusive language and the crying for my dad all followed. Might sound familiar to some of you that wee scenario, if it does then perhaps the drink doesn't suit you either.

The following morning, I woke with a feeling in my stomach that was to be with me for the rest of my drinking days. Of course, at the time of my first drink I had no idea that I was an "alcoholic", or that when I drank alcohol it created a reaction in me that turned me from Dr Jekyll into Mr. Hyde. I could hear my aunt and uncle in the living room and had the fear. Fifteen years old and I had the fear already. I could hear my auntie lamenting about the fact she had brought me on holiday and I was steaming drunk, and she was blaming herself. I prepared for the worst, and got out of bed still with the knot in my belly. That fuckin knot that followed me for 20 years and still to this day rears its ugly head. Fear and Loathing.

"Good morning." She said.

"Morning."

"One question James," she said. "Did you take anything else last night as well as the wine you drank?"

"No I didn`t, Margaret."

"Are you sure? Because you drank about a bottle of wine and were legless, sick, abusive, and crying for your dad." Margaret said to me.

"No. I took nothing else." I was able to answer her with the truth. A word that became foreign to me as the years went by.

She looked at me with love in her eyes and told me straight, "You have to be careful with the drink James, it's not for some people."

That was all she said to me, no bother and no row from her, just telling me that I had to be careful. I know today that she had some insider information on my family and was just looking out for her nephew who she loved with all her heart. All my adult life she pulled me out of one hole or another and she is one of the few folk I care for back in Scotland. At the moment she isn't keeping to well and sometimes I wish I could just go and visit her.

So that was my introduction to alcohol, and funnily enough it had put me off the stuff. I didn't like spinning rooms, being sick, and crying for the father I could barely remember. I didn't drink again for almost 2 years until I had left school some 18 months later. I was sickened by it and didn`t like it, so it was easy to stop taking it.

When I left school, this changed for me though. I started hanging about with the local street gang and starting drinking with them. At first it would just be the weekend, but this soon gradually worked its way into my life in an everyday fashion. I worked for Campbell`s during the day and at night got drunk with my new mates, the gang. We were the Bundy and I still to this day associate myself with the word Bundy. We were following a tradition of 20 years and some have continued it even if only in name some 30 years later. Meadowbank Thistle didn't last that long I don't think.

What began as a couple of cans of lager at the weekend soon became 4 cans and a bottle of cider, then the cider turned to vodka and the weekend soon became Monday to Friday, then the real weekend started. I was making a fair pay at my plumbing game but it was all going on drink, my mum rarely got her dig money on a Friday, and I eventually turned into a monster. I wasn't a full time monster of course, trainee alcoholics and the full blown version I suppose have their alter egos. The one that they show people and the other that only comes out at night and is generally only shown to and affects the people they love and care about.

Well it didn't take long for the police to become a part of my life, a part they are still playing almost 30 years later, although now it's not through alcohol they are involved but because of my involvement in the drug business. I don't particularly care who I offend by this next statement but most policemen are proper cunts, the concept of "the police force" is one that is required, but the organisations themselves are all bent as fuck, and a nice policeman who is conscientious and doing his job for the right reasons is few and far between. That said, I'm not one of the All Coppers Are Bastards group.

My first run in with the Strathclyde Police came in 1982 and was alcohol induced. Two of their finest were arresting one of the Bundy, Steven Tinney, on Castlemilk Drive, and we didn't take kindly to that so we attempted to rescue him. I must say we did free that man and, in my opinion, the two policemen received the kicking that their treatment of the lad deserved. I say we but I doubt if - no I know fine well I didn't - I even got a punch or a kick in at any of them. I left that sort of thing to big Dub and the rest of the lads who actually liked fighting. I did fight but was not very good at it and not that keen either, but I did my bit when required.

The result was the "prisoner" got away and we all made good our escape too. All in separate directions of course, but the majority made their way to my mum's house. I didn't at that point but when I did eventually get there, chaos had ensued.

All the gang had fled back to my mum's house, that was the normal thing for us to do at that time, but now with the benefit of years of hindsight and having to some extent grown up I now think that was wrong. We should have stayed away from my house, my ma`s house. The thing about it is that was the way it was in them days, our mas didn't want us being arrested so they hid us from the polis, plain and simple as that.

Well the polis knew that was one of the places we would have been likely to go, so that's the first place they went to get us. As I wasn`t in the house this is second hand, but the polis had just gathered and kicked my ma`s door off the hinges more or less, then arrested everyone who was in the house at that time, not me cause I wasn`t there remember. They lifted 7 of my mates from the house then hid in the close for me to come back home. Half an hour later when I thought we were safe, that's just what I did, went home. We lived in the ground floor flat, so as I walked up the close two big bastards jumped on top of me and manhandled me to the ground. Yes, I had been there when the polis got battered, and I suppose that made me complicit in the crime, but I hit no one and committed no breach of any peace, perhaps with the benefit of my own pre-edit I would have to admit to the breach of peace. They dragged me from the close and bundled me in to the polis van, my first time in one of them. Unfortunately, it was not to be my last.

Remember, I had just started my new job so the last thing I really wanted was to be arrested and charged with some sort of crime during my 6-week trial period. They drove me down to the old Craigie Street police station and proceeded to charge me with police assault, breach of the peace, and resisting arrest.

I could have cried that night; there are probably those who would say I did. Maybe I did, but it would have been that old thing I did every time I got pissed; I was sick and cried my eyes out. It was not unusual to see me crying when I was drunk at all. Again, there might be some among you who recognise that particular trait in themselves when drunk. Normal drinkers don't just cry when they have had a few, so if that describes you then ask yourself the question.

Anyhow at the bar, the front desk of the Police Station, and not to be confused with a liquor selling establishment, the duty Sergeant deemed me too drunk to be released till morning, so I spent my first night in police custody at the age of seventeen and it was the itchy blanket on the concrete floor. You also got a mattress in them days, but my memory of them is they stank of piss and weren`t very nice at all. I don't really have any memory of the night in the cells, but I do recall not liking it and shitting myself in case I lost my job which I had just started, fuckin murder that was.

On the Sunday morning, the policeman in charge came round and told me to get my gear together because I was being released. Was I happy? Yes, I sure as hell was.

They let me out and told me what I was being charged with, and that I was to appear in front of the Sheriff (for our non-Scottish readers, a Sheriff in Scotland is a lower court Judge) on the following Thursday. Once again I projected forward to my job and the fact that I was on this trial and I would be sacked.

At the time of getting that job I didn't realise I had the ability to do things for myself, I wanted that job so I walked in and walked back out with it. Simple. Now it was looking more like I was going to lose the job and if that happened I would become one of Maggie's one in ten, another number on the list.

On leaving the police station, I could not believe my eyes, every single person who had been arrested the night before was standing outside waiting on my release. They were all slapping me on the back and telling me well done for keeping my mouth shut, and then we walked the couple of miles back up the hill to Castlemilk singing Bundy songs and finishing off our carryout, which in those days the police gave you back. No joking either. We all marched up the hill singing and drinking, me like I was not about to lose my job that Thursday when the Sherriff gave me whatever sentence he decided to hand down to me when I went to court.

And that was that. No beating from the coppers although they could have been a bit gentler with me I'm sure, my only concern was my work. I needn't have bothered.

I went into work on the Monday morning and informed my supervisor that I was going to need the day off that coming Thursday. His name was George Cassidy, and I can still see the look on his face when we spoke that day.

"What do you need the day off for?"

"Well I got into some bother on Saturday night and have to appear in front of the Sherriff on Thursday."

"What kind of bother? He asked.

"Breach of the peace, resisting arrest, and police assault." was my reply.

He just burst out laughing. "Look at the size of you James."

"Good luck and let us know how you get on." Was all he said to me.

"Is that it George?" I enquired.

"Who the fucks going to believe that a wee cunt like you battered any polis?" He laughed.

Never before had I been so happy to see someone laughing at my size and fighting ability. Aye, he`s dead right, I was thinking as I walked away

Thursday came and I was shiteing myself; everyone else had already faced police charges so they couldn`t have cared any less if the judge had sent them down or fined them or whatever the Sherriff decided to do. It was one big laugh to them, but I was not amused at all.

The Sherriff put the case back 2 weeks because a couple of the lads had more serious charges to face, and he wanted to see them out of the road before he dealt with our trial.

There were seven of us accused of the same charges, and the clerk of the court read out all our names starting from the youngest to the oldest. He went along the line calling out our names and as he called out the last name, one of our number called out “HOUSE”. The court went into an uproar. The officials did not think it very funny and I was just mortified, could not believe these cunts thought it was so funny.

Two weeks later we all trooped back up, and by this time big Whitey (Al Dub) had been given 18 months, and one of the other lads had been given 3 years for serious assaults, so they took the blame for the carry on that night in Castlemilk Drive and I was acquitted and allowed to return to my work and tell everyone all about it. This time most likely, with more than a hint of bravado welded onto the tale.

None of us were angels, but essentially we weren’t a bad lot either. There were folk hurt that didn`t need to have been for sure, but most of the violence was against other gangs if you like. I`m not saying this is right, but it was fight or flight, and in a gang fight most people fought, not all of them did right enough, and those who ran will know they did. None of it matters now anyhow. Yesterday is history. Though at this point I’ll spare the embarrassment of anyone who might have ran away when I got bashed up Mitchelhill flats, but you know who came back to rescue me and who didn’t.

What we did do, and it is something that I am not too proud of, is we made the lives of the good folk of Bogany Terraces a total misery, and it would bring me shame some of the shite things I did when I was growing up in that street if I dwelled on it too long.

I`ll give you all an example of something so shite that I still cringe when I think of it even today almost 30 years later. It was the days of the CB radio, good buddy and all that shite. Well if you remember the TV aerials were on the roofs in those days and not sat dishes on walls like today. One of my next close neighbours had a CB and had the King of CB aerials, the Silver Rod, on her roof. The problem arose when they put their Silver Rod on the roof which also happened to house my mum`s TV aerial. When they were putting the rod up they knocked my Mum`s picture off, and me and one of my mates went to the door to ask them to fix it.

"Fuck off, we didn`t touch your aerial." Was the reply from the female who opened the door.

No doubt she would have been given a right mouthful and told what was going to happen, but she couldn`t have cared less because she was getting married in a few days. A wee name calling session ensued but nothing came of it, our aerial didn't get sorted and she prepared for her wedding. We wouldn't have been invited anyway, so the wedding meant fuck all to me and ma big mate. We`d just have carried on watching the 3 channels pished when we were at home at all.

The shite thing happened a few days later on the day of the wedding. I've let go of most of my past, but this one I think about from time to time. So does the guy who was with me because we have spoken about it on Facebook recently.

The family was like the rest of us in the street at that time and didn't have much in the way of money or anything else that could be considered a luxury. That said, they did have a Silver Rod and my aerial was a wee shitty magmount attached to a biscuit tin, hmmm.

So the wedding was a small affair with the reception back in the house in Bogany Terrace. The house was crowded with people celebrating the wedding of one of the girls of the house. I can't even remember the lassies name, but what I do remember is this. My friend and I thought that it would be an ideal time for getting the cunts back for making our TV fuzzy so we hatched a plan that beggars belief.

The wedding reception in the poor people's house was in full swing; they had spent all they had I suppose on making this the special day of their daughter's life.

We went round the back of the building, and with bags of shite and flour and anything we could put into a bag at the time, we smashed all the back windows of the house before throwing the contents of our wee wedding present through their windows. We didn't wait to fight anyone, we fuckin ran away - big men eh? The boy who was with me is filled with shame at this incident as well, but I don't think it would be right to put big Whitey's name in print for something so heinous as smashing the back windows of folk just having a wedding celebration and enjoying themselves.

There was a slight comeback some time later when one of the bride's friends came to my door to shoot me, but I wasn't at home and I'm more than 100% sure this guy didn't have a gun anyway (1982), but I had been bang out of order so who knows. I had friends who knew him, and they spoke to him about speaking to my ma about shite at her door. He was warned not to dare go near my door again and he didn't. That was the end of that one, but just one of those shite occasions that I caused wee Agnes concern. I was 17 then. I`m fuckin 30 years older now and still causing her fuckin grief. Cunt.

I met the people from that family many times over the years and could only offer my apologies to them, apologies which they accepted with the passing of time. Shame on me and the boy who was with me at the time.

So basically that's what we were at that point, a shower of anti-social delinquents who had no regard for anyone's property or in fact no regard for anyone. Of course we had more than our fair share of gang fights but we were a nuisance to the people who lived in and worked from that street, the street we thought belonged to us. We were the first of the wee gangs that destroyed Bogany Terrace. Fact.

It doesn`t make you hard if you think it's funny to turn over some guy's car who has been out fucking working all his days, but I used to thrive on that sort of shite. A wee bastard who would think nothing of putting his boot through your windscreen in the name of the Bundy. Not one single bit of consideration for anyone who might not have had the money to put the window back in the car again.

Now you'd think at some point round about here there would have been some sort of correlation between the facts that I only caused bother when I had consumed the dreaded alcohol. I say dreaded, but I fully understand that it's no problem for lots of folk and fair play to the person who can go out and have a few pints. Fair play even to the person who goes out and has a bucket full but causes no problems anyplace he or she goes. It's when alcohol begins to have an effect on people you are round about, or even folk you come into random contact with, that you should consider it to be at least becoming a problem. I should have known a long time before I was thirty-four and eventually stopped, but there are plenty of stories between me being a seventeen-year-old delinquent who thought he could drink and me stopping alcohol consumption, while in fact alcoholism, or whatever it is that made me act the way I did, was in my blood from way back.

And basically that's how it continued for a few years; I'd work and get drunk. Would give my poor mum fuck all dig money and cause fucking murder at any given opportunity. I was just one angry wee boy who thought he was definitely the man of the house now, and crashed about my mum`s house like it was my own with scant regard for the fact that she was still struggling with two boys, one seventeen who thought he was mad, and the other one who was only twelve and gradually beginning to think he was madder than his daft big brother. Life around our house was never dull, and when Martin reckoned he was old enough, our arguments became serious fighting between two brothers. But our love for one another could never be questioned, and when Martin died a bit of me died as well. But that's all it was, a part of me died with him. I`ll speak about Martins death and the way I didn't deal with it later in the story, but for now it's still the early years and it's the years when I began to take drugs.

Chapter 2: Highs and Lows

This book is written neither to condone nor to condemn drug taking, but in my opinion people should be allowed to put whatever they like into their own bodies. If they want to smoke some hash let them, if they want to take heroin let them. Why does the guy who has smoked only a joint feel in the position to judge someone who has taken heroin? The guy who has been sniffing cocaine for 20 years but looks down his nose at the guy who uses heroin. Some sort of inverted drug snobbery I call it. And I hope to be able to explain to you all in the next few pages why that is my outlook on the drug scene, coming from the perspective of someone who grew up not surrounded by alcohol and drug misuse. I should point out that I saw neither in my house until I began to bring them in.

Most of the best music ever written was written by song writers who had taken LSD or had been smoking pot or taking heroin. That is a fact that cannot be denied by anyone. Pink Floyd, Neil Young, and The Beatles all wrote songs with a drug element in them, and to say Bob Marley might have been smoking some grass when he was creating his music is like saying there might be snow on the top of Mount Everest so wrap up well for the climb.

Drugs inspire a lot of people to be more creative, which cannot be denied. Having said that, I am fully aware that drugs ruin lots of people's lives and will continue to do for as long as people keep taking them, without due care and attention, and without being fully informed of the dangers, whatever those dangers may be. There is also the fact that the very illegality of these substances means that they are controlled by organised crime – and all the shite that goes with that like human trafficking – and there is no control over the quality of what hits the streets. Go look into the details of drug deaths and see how often a death is down to the shite these scumbags cut substances with. I just believe that they are a fact of life and people should be allowed to make an informed choice of their own about whether they should or should not take them.

So back to me anyway and my own introduction was through acid or LSD. No gateway of cannabis or any shite like that. Cannabis is not a gateway drug, and it does not lead anyone to taking anything they wouldn't take anyway. That was one of the anti-drugs, police led campaigns of the 80s that they came up with or certainly championed.

So I started taking LSD with my mates and we had some laughs, but that was all it was to us; there was no Carlos Castaneda and the Teachings of Don Juan for us lot. At that point we really were not into expanding our minds or any of that shit. We took the drug for the fun of it. It was about the colours and the ever changing shapes of faces and the hysteria that surrounded LSD that we loved. We would be lying looking at clouds or down in the woods at Bogany or up Cathkin Braes having some laugh. It was a great time for me, finding this mind altering substance that didn't make me want to go out and fight with anyone. I continued to take LSD or Acid as it's known for years to come.

Then I progressed on to what the anti-drug campaigners would call hard drugs. Well I suppose in heroin that is exactly what I got. When I was eighteen, I dabbled in that "magical brown powder from the east" for about six or seven months, and during that time I loved that as well. Incidentally, it was Bez in his book who called it "that magical brown powder from the east" when he spoke about his own battle with smack.

Mine was no battle though, and my involvement came about by total accident. I didn't set out to try heroin but one Saturday night that's what happened. I tried smack for the first time; it was an experience that I will never forget even 30 years later.

Me and two of my mates had decided to try speed, we had never tried that either by this point but were ready to give it a go and see how it went. We chipped in a total of £10 and sent one of the gang to get the stuff. Now anyone who has waited and waited on the drugs coming will understand that it can be some waiting process and one that stretched the nerves for as far as they will go.

Our man who went to get the stuff that night I'm going to call Dumper to save his real name from being made public, but anyone who knows me knows Dumper, and anyone who has any idea that I dabbled will know who he is and why I called him that. He was and still is a fair bit of a character in Castlemilk, but he was renowned for not returning with the goods he had been sent for, so me and the other guy waited and hoped, that it would not be in vain, for his return.

About an hour later he came back from his own wee adventure and told us he had good news and bad news. The bad news was he could not get us any speed, so you might be able to imagine the downer me and this other bloke were now in on this dry Saturday evening.

“Not to worry lads,” he quickly assured us, “I’ve got us this other gear that everyone is taking. “What do you mean new gear, Dumper?” I asked him.

“Smack” said he.

“You can go and fuck yourself, I’m not taking that shite, have you seen the state of the cunts cutting about the shops on that shite?”. There was a crowd or more than one I suppose who had already began taking heroin, and the local shopping arcade was one of their hang outs. You couldn’t move without someone asking for “Ten Bob” or a quid. It was always to buy a can of beer or a bit of hash, no one ever admitted it was to go and buy heroin. It was so sad at first I reckon; you knew all these folk or their family at least, but had to watch as they turned in to part of Thatcher’s-underclass of zombie smack heads. People made choices, I won't argue they didn't, but it was Thatcher that helped bring about that sub-culture. It had always suited Governments to have the percentage that is messed up. It suited then and it still suits them now.

"Well James, I've bought it now, so what the fuck do you want me to do with it"?

And that is how me, Dumper, and the other lad who will remain unnamed ended up a close snorting smack off a window ledge. He most likely had a bit wherever he had got it from too, because that was his bag throughout our drug taking years together. He was always a greedy bastard and I'm sure if he`s still fighting the battle then he`ll still be a greedy bastard. He always has been and always will be my friend though.

In a big way, we were very fortunate that we hadn't been brought up in a lot of other streets in Castlemilk. I say that because we were the forerunners of the smack take off in Bogany. All the older guys like my cousin Con and his mate Stevie Brown had just missed it and had been going to the dancing for a few years already at this point in my life. They`d have been about 6 years older than us, so we didn't have any negative role models as did most other streets in the Scheme at that time. They were into Bowie and other music, into their clothes and fancy haircuts. Fancy is an operative term for what we thought was pretty fuckin gay to be honest. Turns out they were actually cool as fuck and having the time of their lives like folk should try to do a bit more.

So I reckon in a roundabout way, I have them older lads who became my friends as I too got older for being positive role models, even if they took on those roles unwittingly.

And that was my introduction to heroin; we were snorting it and it was my shot first, like I said Dumper would have already had his wee sniff wherever he had just come from. I put out a wee line on the window sill and snorted the brownish powder, the other two quickly followed, although to be honest, I think the quieter lad was wishing he hadn`t bothered his arse getting involved in our carry on by this point. He'd wanted speed and was now snorting a line of smack from a dirty close window ledge in Bogany Terrace. He most likely cringes at the thought nowadays, but I haven't seen him for years so it doesn't matter much to me anymore anyway.

It was bogging anyway, the taste getting worse as it trickled down the back of our throats and then BANG. The kick off it was immediate. My head began to spin and I'd say at this point I didn`t like it. Then came the best part of it for me anyhow, the projectile vomiting. I was being violently sick and it was easily flying ten yards past us like a scene from The Exorcist, I felt tremendous. Anytime I get the projectile vomit now it reminds me of my heroin days.

They didn’t last that long to be honest, and the reason I did stop was because I couldn`t bear to put a needle into myself or indeed let anyone else do it for me either. The other boy that was with Dumper and I that night most likely didn`t touch the stuff ever again and I’m glad of that. Me and Dumper though got on to it like a pair of addicts, though we both didn`t think we were at that time; we just took anything for the buzz.

I was working in the plumbing trade still, and in the early 80s the Government were giving people who bought the council stock grants to do up their old houses. Money for central heating and lead pipe renewal, amongst other stuff that didn’t bother us plumbers, was being given by the Tory Government to the folk who did buy their Council houses so they could put in the new heating and renew the old pipe work. I was 17/18 by this time and making a small fortune from the scrap we were stealing every second day when we stripped another house.

I was working with this big guy from East Kilbride called Norrie Agnew, and he was very good to me. He was on price work and I was his apprentice, so I made sure all his preparation work was done and then he would fire the heating systems and bathrooms in to the “New” houses. He would always put a few bob extra put into my pay packet, and he would also give me my share of the scrap we were getting almost daily. We used to strip the houses then put the company share in the van and drop it at the yard; they had counted the figures in their projections for the price of the work being done so they had to get some of the scrap back to be included in their profits.

Big Norrie and I, on the other hand, used to strip whatever he told me to strip and off to the scrap yard we would go. Now fuck knows what we were getting at the time, but he would never take me into the yard with him.

“It’s not worth you getting caught and sacked” he`d tell me. Of course, what he was really doing was getting the lion’s share around the corner and giving me my wee drop when he got back to the cafe or pub he`d left me in. To be honest, I was not giving a fuck because between what he was giving me extra for the work I was doing and what I was getting as an apprentice, I was making £250 a week as an 18-year-old, and for 4 months or so it all went on heroin for me and my buddy Dumper. His dad worked for himself and was very good at the job he did, and as is normally expected in them situations, or at least was, Dumper was being lined up to succeed him.

Trouble was, he wasn’t much for working at the time because his dad kept paying him off for stealing one thing or another from which ever job his dad sent him to. The fuckin drugs will do that to you but.

Then came the big day, the day I was going to have my first hit, my first injection of heroin. Me, Dumper, and another lad called Paul had all chipped in £20 between us and were all set for the big darts match.

It was going to be in my mum's house one night while she was at the bingo, my first step into the land of no return, well that was true for most of the lads I knew who took it anyway. I was terrified and when my shot came I declined. I plain and simply shat it.

The smack was in the spoon and it had been filtered ready for it to be pumped into my arm. I could not bring myself to do it, no fucking way.

"Is it ok if I have mine anyway?" said Paul, who was already on the road to hell. He was, and could well still be, an example of one of those folk who shouldn't take drugs.

"Batter in mate, I'm done with that shite for sure" I said to him. Dumper followed him at his back and I gave them my share as well. I had played about with a dangerous drug for six months or so, and I was lucky to be one of the few boys from Glasgow in the early 1980s who got through it at that time, and who was fortunate that one experience had been enough to put me right off the carry on that was heroin.

As I write this, I'm thinking of people close to me who have died as a result of heroin over the years, and also the words I have just written about streets and role models. Some of them were brought up in streets which had no positive role models, their parents worked hard and they wanted for nothing, but on many of those streets, heroin was all the rage, the fashion if you will.

A common story among some of those overdoses was young guys having their final hit with these older guys, and they did that thing that became almost the 'thing to do', they allowed him to die because they were fucked up and in order to protect them from any police charge. Jesus, they could at least have stuck the guy in a taxi or something. Though I never witnessed one of those incidents, I can imagine no much would have been done to help them. That's another fuckin thing the drugs will dae tae ye. Since the mid-1990s, heroin has made a resurgence and I can't understand how the young people of today who would have watched that all those years ago could still be getting into it once again. Mental. I wish them all the best and hope they come through it like I did.

So it was a back to the alcohol for me, although I hadn`t really stopped completely during my time on the smack. I was eighteen years old and getting drunk most nights, the weekend arrests had become more common, and getting locked up two or three times every week was not uncommon to me at that time.

In later years when I went to try getting work in social work, I had over 25 previous convictions. All from the 1980s, and every single one had alcohol involved in the offence, mostly public order offences, assaults, and the standard resisting arrest which Strathclyde Police charged everyone they arrested with. I'm quite sure the figures would tell the story themselves.

So it was back to the streets with some of the gang from before, some of them had gone down the same road as me and some of them were in prison from during my time on the smack. Mostly for offences of violence, and a couple of them had been given 3 and 5 years at the time of my liaison with the brown powder, I didn't fancy that at all.

But things had not changed for me. I still got drunk very easily, still was always sick and never could keep out of trouble. I had started to hang about with some other lads who instead of just hanging about the streets of Castlemilk were heading up the town and spending time at pubs or at the dancing, so my social life had changed somewhat, but not that much to be honest. I was doing this thing that none of my mates did, I got into bother every time I took a drink. Every single time and I kid you not. None of my friends exhibited any sort of this behaviour, the new bunch I was hanging with anyway and I still couldn't see it. I was allergic to alcohol, I was the clown who did all the daft shit and who caused all the bother, and who just changed when he drank. I was fun, some laugh, and great company to be with, but then it would all go upside down somewhere along the line, and in the course of an evening I would start a big fight, or be cheeky to a big guy and get battered, and that led to my mates becoming involved and in general all hell used to break loose around me. I was, of course, not the only one, but it's my book so if anyone else wants to put their hands up to starting it all the time then get writing.

I know one big former bus driver who will be smiling at that line and saying "put the wood in the ole duck".

No one else did to the extreme that I did at least.

My big mate at the time, and still to this day, is called Chris Cleland. He had some family in Jersey in the Channel Islands so we decided to work a bit harder, save up, and head over to Jersey. Plenty of work he told me, birds all over the place he told me, but what he didn't mention although in hindsight he most likely did - was that alcohol was not taxed on Jersey so it cost fuck all to get pished when we eventually got there in April 1985, seems like so long ago. I suppose that`s because it was...

We had it all planned, jobs were being set up for us for getting there, we had a place to stay, and it was going to be just the best times of our young lives. We were going to be earning a fortune and shagging for Scotland.

Big Chris told me so himself and I gave it some thought. We would be working straight away, house all set to go, and the women. Now when I was nineteen, I had the opportunity to have this life. Wow eh.

What I did not take into consideration was the debt I would be leaving behind. Well I did but I thought fuck that. It's not getting paid. Banks and cards, fuck them all I mused. The answer was dead easy. Fuck off. Don't Deal with any of your shit, James. Dead fucking easy. I gave not one jot of a fuck about any debt or the fact that I was just going to leave my apprenticeship which only had seven months to go and I'd have been qualified. Fuck it. I couldn't blame any of that on the fuckin drugs but.

All would be just fine. What I didn't realise and it took me some years to eventually realise, is that +even if I had gone to the moon there would soon have been trouble there for me as well. James Toner and alcohol was not a very good mix.

Jersey was great, and I spent the 2 years I was there doing what I thought was enjoying myself, but which if the truth be told, was far from it. I was drinking most nights and it was in Jersey that my alcohol habit really took off. And the bottom line of it was that the more I drank, the greater the likelihood of me causing bother was. It was as simple as that.

I don't really want to dwell on my time in Jersey too much, but having said that, there were a fair few adventures – and misadventures during my time there. The latter of those only showed just how much a problem I had wi the drink, even if I didnae fully realise it yet. So indulge me for this next chapter while I take a look back at my time on the place we called 'The Rock'.

Chapter 3: Jersey Nights

First of all, I should begin this chapter by telling you that the 2 years I spent in Jersey were two of the finest years I have had in my life. Wine, wummin, and song. I should also be honest, because it's an honest book this, and tell you that I did absolutely no shagging on that island during those 2 years; ma granny stayed too far away tae be saying a shagged birds up her bit. That didn't even work in Glasgow because she only stayed up the stair fae me. Anyway, apparently good looking young birds discriminate against wee fat Scottish guys that didn't measure up, so they didn't give me a fair crack at the whip at all. Tight wee cows we used to call them. That's a play on words in case anyone reading gets confused. All I did was get drunk, get drunker, and cause bother. I experienced my first time in hospital because of the drink in Jersey, I experienced my first bout of penal servitude - the jail- when I was in Jersey, but I had the time of my life doing it. I still had no idea what the problem was.

So this is just a wee brief overview of my time on the Island, or The Rock as it was called. Not the rocks I became heavily involved with in my later years, but it was a small island, and folk used to say it was 60,000 alcoholics clinging to a rock. I was one of them alkies but didn't know it at the time.

In Jersey, as I had been before, I was the clown prince in the pub, everyone having some laugh at my line of shite then BOOM, I'd have a blackout and not be able to recall anything in the morning. More often than not it was down to the pub to find out where the blood came from this time, whether I was barred or not, or if I had to fight the biggest cunt in the place because I was giving him cheek and trying to fire into his wife the night before. I didn't have to fight too many big cunts because sorry was still working at this point.

Every weekend was now every night, and it didn't change in 2 years on that rock.

When Big Chris and I got there, the work that had been promised was not very forthcoming so we had to look for our own work, imagine that, having tae find yer own job. I was soon starting to wish I hadn`t left my cushy wee apprenticeship job and had stayed for the 7 or 8 months I had to go before I was a time served plumber. My arrival on Jersey was a total anticlimax. We had no jobs and no place to stay, so we headed for the small hotel beside the pub that Chris`s Uncle John had told us was his local. You should have seen the state of this fuckin dive; shite hole indeed.

It had a guest house up the stair, so we took a room for a couple of nights, caught up with some sleep, and prepared to start our jobs as soon as before moving into our new gaff. Haha. No Jobs were forthcoming and we had to find a gaff for ourselves. This involved buying the Jersey Evening Post and searching every tea time for some sort of decent accommodation to live in. I wasn't enjoying the real world one wee bit at this point in time.

That said we'd still be out in the pub each and every night, so what did it matter where we stayed to be honest.

Because I was telling the wee white lie that I was a time served plumber, I got work straight away. The guy's name was Colin Tudic and he asked me what I could do. I remember looking at him as if he was daft and telling him I could do anything plumbing associated. This was of course lies but it was horses for courses in the early days in Jersey for me and Chris. Telling lies tae get work for food, drink, and a dry bed at night. Nae borra.

Before long, we got ourselves a wee room in a lady called Mrs. Lock`s house, that is all it was though. A big double room with 2 single beds of course. So at the start of the second week. I started my job with Tudic and Chris, well he just stayed in his bed. He`d have a hard day in front of him looking for work or lying in the park sunning himself, he assured me he was doing both and I wasn`t about to disbelieve him. He ended up looking like a right bronzed Adonis. That was our joke at the time.

The first day on my job and the gaffer, Colin, asked if I could do lead work. I`m no expert, but I can dress the lead down and make things water tight I lied. That's all he wanted to hear, so off we went to this job on the roof of a bank and he showed me what was required. As soon as he'd left the roof I lay down and caught 40 winks. For one thing I was tired, and the other was I didn`t have one clue what was expected of me on that roof. I lay about all day and did nothing. Colin came back at half 4ish and asked what I'd done.

"Well the truth is Colin, I don't do lead work and I was just a bit embarrassed telling you that", now that was the truth so what was his problem then.

"You won`t be getting paid for sitting up here doing fuck all day he said to me" he growled.

"No Colin, I didn`t think I would have been".

"We'll keep you on till the end of the week, and if you can do anything I`ll keep you on".

"£30 a shift and don't be expecting anything for today".

"Fair enough Colin, I won't let you down". At the end of the week he gave me my pay packet with £120 pounds in it and told me my services were no longer required.

Truth be told, I shouldn't have expected anything else from the guy, he was trying to run a business and not some charity for runaway Scottish boys, but the reality was I fuckin hated him. I carried a resentment against about for the next 30 odd years, fuck.

Don’t worry, there is plenty of work in the island and just try and be honest with the guy who is giving you the job, tell him your time is just out and he`ll take you on as an improver, sort of someone who hasn’t finished their time and who needs a bit of time to find his feet. Tellin maself like.

Don’t remember that beardy bastard offering me the chance to improve with them at all, take your tools and thanks for your service. Maybe he could see that I was not the man for improving in the plumbing trade and felt he`d only be wasting both our times. Big resentment there. All born from me lying and being a shite plumber.

So that night I went to the Great Union pub after my work and sat with my face tripping me and wishing I had stayed in Glasgow. My wages were in the bank if I was at my work or not, and I had practically no outlays in terms of food or any of that stuff at the time.

“Why had I come to this fucking Island?” I still had no idea. I was running away from the monster that was me and alcohol. A very heady mix indeed, but didn’t take me long to find that out.

So I’m sitting in the Great Union pub this Friday afternoon, and in walks this bloke who I knew from playing pool in the bar with. His name is Eddie Rennie; he came from a wee place just outside Glasgow called Holytown.

"Alright wee man, what's up wi your face this fine Friday Night?", he chirped. It was the chirp of a man who had just been paid and was going out on the razzle that night, and most likely for the whole of the weekend at that point.

"Got paid aff today by that cunt, Colin Tudic." was all I could manage

"Is your time out".

"No Eddie, I chucked it with 7 months to go and headed over here with ma mate".

"The big ginger cunt"?

"Aye."

"Is he working?"

"He`s getting some kitchen work but we`ll get on our feet soon enough".

"Would you do anything else for work wee man?" Eddie asked.

At this stage when two Scottish men are speaking about work and shit, the conversation generally turns to talk of sucking cocks or the like.

"Almost anything Eddie" I said smiling. I knew then that he had taken to me, because my humour was as bad as his and he had most likely been in the same position a hundred times before.

"Leave it with me wee man and I'll sort you something out" he carried on speaking and with an air of a man who was enjoying life. Jersey looked like it was being good to him, and he looked like the guy who was going to be going out that night and returning home not alone. Getting his hole, I'm sure.

"Leave it wi me till Monday and I'll get something sorted for you wee man".

And that's exactly what he did, left it till Monday and got me something sorted out.

Again I was sitting in the Great Union and in walks Eddie about 3ish I`d reckon.

"Alright wee man. Are you feeling any better?"

"To be honest, not really Eddie, I'm skint, hungry, and could be doing with a beer" I told him with the honesty I felt.

He walked to the bar and brought me a can of Grolsch, my drink of choice at that time.

"Right that's you got a tab behind the bar for your food in here too, just pay it on a Friday and you won't ever go hungry."

"Just the job now and I'll be sorted Eddie, thanks for the beer and setting up the dinner tab, appreciated".

"Oh ah forgot to tell you that you're working with us from tomorrow if you want too".

Eddie was a roof tiler and he had got me a start with his boss labouring for them.

I really could not believe that this guy who didn't really know me had done all this out of the kindness of his heart, they obviously needed a labourer and I fitted the bill, so they had given me the job. I was well made up that I had another job so soon and wouldn`t be sitting about the pubs waiting on someone dropping a job on my lap. The arrangements for the pick up the next morning were made and I continued drinking the beer Eddie had bought me. He`d given me a £10 sub too, so when Chris eventually turned up we both did the usual thing that folk in Jersey did then and most likely still do. We just got drunk.

Next morning, I was at the pickup point ready to start my new job labouring to these two slaters. Keen as fuckin mustard I was. The gaffers name was Rab Bone and anyone I speak to from the old Jersey days doesn't have anything nice to say about that cunt for sure.

Anyhow I thought he was some man, he`d given me a job and here on the first morning was taking me and Eddie for our breakfast. Into some cafe and ordered 3 brekkies and 3 teas. Couldn't believe it at all. Rab was from Ayr in Scotland but he must have been run out of that town, I reckoned by the end of the week.

He took me and Eddie to the job and showed me what he wanted me to do; carry tiles up a ladder was part of it, remember I'm this wee fat cunt wi nae strength eh. I began my work with Eddie in knots at the state of me trying to load tiles on to this roof from a ladder, but the sweat was pouring and it must have been doing me some sort of good. That's what Eddie told me anyway. We couldn`t have been on the job an hour when Bone made good his escape telling us he`d see us for lunch.

Eddie didn't work me hard and as long as he wasn`t waiting on me then he was happy enough. Eddie was 6 foot and could fight like fuck. One of them cunts who can fight and who enjoys it as well, dangerous if you're on the other side of that. Anyway Bone turns up about 1 and shouts us down from the roof, dinner time boys he said.

We left the job and headed towards the nearest pub which sold food, no alcohol during the day when we were on the roofs but I was being fed my second dinner of the day so I wasn't bothered too much about alcohol or any of that shit, not until the shift was over at least.

After dinner Bone did the same thing, took me and Edie to the job and fucked off and left us to it. Sometimes we would be held up and Eddie told me some of his tales of Jersey and beyond. He was some man. He had this little stammer and when he got drunk so did the stutter, I think Eddie`s Mum could have saved a few broken noses and jaws if she had taken her boy for some speech therapy when he was younger. He got angry, stuttered a little bit more, then the punches and karate kicks started. I am awfully glad that I didn't ever get in to his bad books, not once in 2 years. Not bad that for me in those days either.

So this continued until the end of the week when Bone didn't turn up to collect us to bring us back home to the Union. These were pre mobile days of course so tracking him down proved no mean feat for Eddie, but I knew Bone was scared of him and getting our wages would be no problem at all. Eddie tried to call all his local haunts but we couldn't track him down. In his rage Eddie`s stammer was getting fu fu fuckin worse and he promised me he would kill him when he got him. I had not one reason to disbelieve him.

Our rage was made all the worse by the fact we had to get 2 buses back into town before Eddie began looking in his local pubs to find the cunt. I needed my wages and I needed them that night. I had my dinner bill behind the bar in the Union to pay, and had also borrowed some money to go for a beer during the week. Eddie tried one more call; I was not in the box but I knew he had gotten hold of Bone. I could see the angry face and the missed out words together with the repetition of the involuntary sounds that folk with stammers do.

"We`ve to get him in the Bristol at 8" Eddie fumed.

"Are we getting paid Eddie"?

"Don't you worry wee man, that prick will never fuck you for your wages as long as I'm working with him".

As I thought about the relationship between the pair of them, I could see Eddie had no fear for him, in fact it was more like contempt.

So Eddie and I met in the Union about 7 and had a few pints, cans of Grolsch in my case. We walked down to the Bristol just before 8 and there at the pool table was Rab Bone, smiling through his teeth and gaining no favour with me. He may have been older than me and might well have given me a doin, but I would have had no hesitation in battering the head off the cock with a pool cue. No fuckin problem. Get the wages out, I thought to myself, but was allowing Eddie to do any talking that was required in this situation. One I had never encountered in my life before, my pay for the weeks work I had just done wasn`t there. Fuck sake man. Eddie looked like he was ready to explode.

“Well boys, just skelped that cunt for £1500 quid”. He had been playing the other guy for our wages.

He pulled a bundle out of his pocket and counted off a bundle before giving it to Eddie.

“Right wee man, how many shifts did you do this week”?

“Four.” I replied.

“Right there you go then, that’s us all square and I’ll see you on Monday morning again”.

I looked at the money he had put in my hand and then looked at him.

"Are you having a laugh Rab?".

"How, what's up? "He sneered.

"Well I've worked 4 shifts and you've given me £60".

"I didn't ask you to." I said to him when he quoted the fact that he had bought me breakfast and lunch all week.

"You've given me 60 quid. Once I pay my bill at the Union and my rent money, I'm left with fuck all, that's wrong Rab".

He looked at Eddie who sort of moved his head in agreement with what I had just said.

"Ok, is another £5 a shift good enough for you wee man?"

"It's better than getting nothing at all and having to watch you playing cunts at pool for my wages, but still not ideal is it?"

"Cool then." He gave me the extra £20 quid and told me to meet them on Monday at the same time and place. I was in no position to argue with him so I just took what was mine and told him I'd see him on the Monday.

I felt as long as Eddie was there I would always be paid and it was a good laugh working with him too. Ah had to tell Eddie a few shagging lies because he took a different bird home with him every night he went out. So I made up a few wee tales of my own, but I had to be on my toes cos he knew I was at it. The big bastard was always trying to catch me out, and that wouldn't have done my ever growing credibility in the Union any good whatsoever.

So my life in Jersey wasn`t that bad. I moved from job to job till I got another chance at the plumbing again. During the time between plumbing jobs, I worked with Eddie and in between did some bar work. At the time I thought I was mad, but didn't quite realise that I actually had this aversion to alcohol that not everyone else had. I was an alcoholic in the making and just didn't know it.

My mate Dumper who had introduced me to heroin was still fighting a losing battle, and in a phone call his father asked me if he could come over and spend some time with me on Jersey in the hope that his heroin habit could not be fed, because in 1985 there was no Heroin on the Island. The Scousers soon put a change to that, in my opinion only of course. The first time I saw anything akin to smack was Dicanol, a strong pain killer that actually killed one of my friends over there. His girlfriend who gave him the injection was given 2 years Borstal in England for that. So Mr. Dumper asked me if it would be ok if he sent his boy over for me to look after him so to speak. Dumper had been my mate for years and I didn't understand that whatever his problems, he`d be taking them with him to wherever he went. This time it was to me in Jersey. I`m not sure how long he actually lasted, but it was mayhem from the word go when he did get there. He was out creeping offices and stealing and any shit he could get his hands on. I`m talking handbags and shit he was stealing here. Sometimes I even went as lookout, but to be honest I was shite at that sort of thing. Out and out stealing has never been my bag, but I have taken shit that doesn`t belong to me and not given it back, same thing really.

So he was earning his living blagging bags and sharing the proceeds with me and Chris, let's not forget that either. I was moving from pillar to post, and doing anything that came up and sometimes had money and sometimes didn't. The only difference about being skint in Glasgow and being skint in Jersey is no mammy there to pull you out of the hole you had dug for yourself. Basically when you were skint on Jersey then you were skint full stop.

So I had work most of the time, but it was the age old story of subbing it all through the week and having none left on payday. Life was full of deathers and dirty dives as they were called back in the day, and they are as they sound. Stay in the pub till the death was called - a deather - and a dirty dive was when you had finished your deather and you went home to your bed and had a dirty dive. Straight into bed with the working gear on and not a wash in sight, washed your face in the morning and your pits, but it was common in my time not to give a fuck about cleanliness, during the week at any rate.

Chris had jumped ship and moved back in with his old bird, and he wouldn`t listen to us. So me and Dumper used to get pished together and in fact we had moved into this nice wee gaff close to town together too, and all was well. That`s to say until someone gave Dumper Valium which he was taking with his drink. I`d be a liar if I said I hadn't taken a few myself, but not to the extent that he was taking them. In the book 'Shantaram', the author is speaking about Australian jails and he calls certain types of people "stand over merchants". Dumper was one of these people. A bully of sorts who thought he deserved his share of whatever was going about, whether it be sweeties, drink, or drugs. I only mention this to try and explain where he`d have been getting his valium from. So one night we were in the Great Union pub when all of a sudden Dumper, who could be volatile at times, stood up and launched this big heavy ashtray at someone on the other side of the room. It missed its intended target but all hell broke loose in the pub; he`d managed to start an old fashioned cowboy fight in this small pub in Jersey. Mayhem ensued, people getting hit with glasses and chairs and all sorts. Dumper got put out of the pub that night but I decided to stay because it was him that started and caused it once again. Normally it would be me that was on the other side of the pub door with my mates still warming themselves inside getting even drunker.

Dumper was never one to fuck about though and it wasn't long before the windows of the pub started to come in on top of the place, Dumper was going round the pub with his stick or whatever he had and smashing every window in the place. If you think about it, that`s what delinquents do and I don't think delinquency starts or stops at any age. The pub emptied and most of the locals got Dumper to the ground and held him there till the police arrived on the scene, Cannae really blame them though, eh. Soon the place was blue wi policemen, and Dumper was taken away to spend the night in the cells before he appeared in the court in the morning.

The Judge gave him a fine with the alternative to leave the Island; having no money the choice was quite simple. Deported from Jersey, never to return.

They gave him a few days to get off the Island and that was that. I was in sort of 2 minds about the full thing. He was a liability because of his narcotic intake and the fact he was just as mad if not madder than me, but he was my pal and had been since school days. He still is to this day in fact. So we went to the pub, another one, to get pissed and to plan for the exit party. I think we had got him a flight on the Sunday, so we decided to cut things neat and had the party on the Saturday night.

We went to a place called Fort Regent, and in Fort Regent was this club that had these nights where you spent £5 to get in and drank all you could to your heart's content all night. I was on the Vodka and fresh orange, and although I'm in no doubt the drink would have been watered down a touch, I still ended up blootered. Absolutely paralytically drunk. I have no memory of leaving that club or what really happened next but I do know that I got myself into my first bit of bother on Jersey. It wasn`t to be my last of course, bother came to me without me even trying to find it. Only this night I was on the lookout for bother, in any shape or form.

That night I took the shape of some retarded pseudo car thief. I couldn't even drive, but I had this thing when I was drunk that I liked to sit in cars pretending to drive them. This was quite easy in Jersey because no one locks up their cars on the Island. That I was lucky enough to find an open car with the keys still in it. Would you believe that.

So there I am cutting about with a pink polo shirt on and having it in every car I came upon. I was going into them, and if they were fast cars I`d sit and pretend to go fast, gear changes the lot. If they were not worthy of me driving them, I would just rifle the car for any old shite that I could find in them. Cassette tapes, gloves, umbrellas, packets of chewing gum. All easy prey for this not at all professional shite car thief.

I`m sure you are already getting a wee picture of the state I was in. Could hardly stand, but still was in and out of every car in this giant car park. I was taking the stuff I was stealing from the cars back to my flat, the flat I shared with Dumper who was being put off the island in the morning. My bed was like a veritable Aladdin`s cave of shite. You name it, and I had stolen it from these cars that were unlocked. Hank Marvin and Roy Orbison tapes. Ladies' and gents' umbrellas, Hats, scarves and almost anything else you can think that some idiot would be taking as a trophy back to his flat after taking it out of a car that didn't belong to them. Well not this one, I made run after run after run. My room was so full of shite that when Dumper woke up to go to the airport in the morning he would have some laugh. That was the object of my carry on. Nothing more or less than that, me having a laugh but alcohol driven. But no one else was in on this laugh, just me.

I made one last attempt to see what I could find and found Christmas had come early to me. An open van with the keys inside already for me to shoot away in, vroom vroom, I revved her up.

Problem was I couldn`t drive, never had in my life driven a car. This was to be my first shot where the vroom vroom was real.

I got the car into 1st gear, and shot across the road into a petrol pump, smash. I of course didn't hang about too long to see what the outcome would be, but to be totally honest I hardly made good my escape when I had the fuckin chance. I was picked up 5 minutes later with a big pair of leather gauntlet gloves on and carrying a big set of keys that the turnkey at Aitkenhead Road would have been proud of.

"Hello Son." said one policeman.

"Where have you been?" He asked looking at my oil covered pink top and my leather gauntlets that I still had on.

“I was walking my bird up the road” I said.

“You both working late like?” said one of them.

I was invited into the Police car and driven round the corner to the garage I had crashed into.

The copper looked at me. “Son, you were lucky to walk away from that smash.”

“You are right” I said to the Policeman. “What now”.

“Where do you live son?” They asked. I told them, and we agreed to a search of my premises. Bad idea I know, but I wasn’t thinking very sharply at this point anyway.

So we go back to the apartment that I’m sharing with Dumper who leaves for Scotland first thing in the morning. He is woken by the room light going on; an unwritten law between us was that the light was not put on when any of us came in later than the other.

“For fuck sake James” He muttered.

“Wasn`t me that put it on this time Dumper.”. Talkin boot the light.

He had one look up at the mess that surrounded him then another at the Policemen with me in handcuffs and used his intuition to put 2 and 2 together.

“What have you done”?

“You working for them now” I asked, smiling.

“He`s been acting like a fuckin idiot and he`s lucky to be alive” said one of the policemen.

“And how am a lucky being alive mate?” I asked.

“You hit the fucking petrol pump, James. It could have exploded and you would have gone up in flames with it”.

To be honest, that had not crossed my mind till that point and I just shook my head in a downward manner.

“What’s going to be happening to him then?” Dumper wanted to know.

“We’ll be taking him to the police station and trying to find out what he`s been up to.” One of the policemen told him.

“I`m leaving on the first flight in the morning” Dumper told them.

“That’s ok pal this has nothing to do with you lad”.

And that was the last time I saw my mate Dumper for about 18 months; he went back to Scotland and I went with the policemen to the police station.

I was charged with various offences and bailed to appear at another time before the same bloke who had sentenced Dumper, Centenier Le Broq. He was a bit of a well-known “sheriff” type figure from Jersey who handed out some pretty stiff sentences, especially against non-islanders. He gave me a date to go back and bailed me to appear at a further date.

I now had two problems; one was that my landlord wasn`t going to be very happy that his house had been invaded by the Old Bill last night, and the lady who was in charge of the pub I was working in would perhaps be pissed off as well at me.

Obviously the first thing I did was to go to the pub to see if I still had job in the bar.

"Don't be silly darling, of course you have luv." She told me. Her name was Babs, and there was always some ambiguity as to whether Babs was a man or a woman. That morning I really couldn't have cared less, because she had told me that my job was safe, and with a drunk driving case in Jersey an automatic prison sentence was likely on the cards for you.

I was happy at that, so I sat down and had a wee drink at the bar. That first drink led to the next, and then before I knew it I was pished and had no intent on going back to see the landlord to see what he thought about the fiasco of the night before. Powerless.

I didn`t give a fuck about that man or his wife, or the fact that their house had been invaded by the police and their privacy had been violated by something they had no control over at all. I just got drunk; 'I'll go see him tomorrow.' In my head he was only going to throw me out anyway, so what`s the point in heading round to see him right away.

Manners is the word I had forgotten all about by this point in my drinking career, fuck him and his daft wife.

Only had a few beers and the fuck everyone attitude was back on. Shite that was.

While me and Dumper had lived in that house, there was one other drunken incident that is maybe worth mentioning. I woke in the morning covered in oil or grease shit.

“What went on last night then, Dumper?” I asked as I opened the curtains of our room. There was no need for him to answer because I already knew.

“You climbed right to the top of that last night, ya mad bastard”

Across the road from our gaff was the local gasworks, and I had climbed up the big blue gas meters that we see around the cities of the UK, and further afield too I’d imagine.

Flashback immediately.

“Why didn’t you try to stop me”? I asked him.

“Ah did, but you started fighting with me and I didn’t see the point of a big fight, so I came halfway up with you”.

I smiled and we had a laugh, but some place deep down in the pit of my stomach I knew that was wrong. I knew that I was putting my life and more than likely other folks' lives in danger. I always told that story as one of my mad funny ones, but I knew that it wasn`t the things that other people were doing on their way home from pubs and clubs. I think at that point I was starting to feel something was different from me and everyone else who could have 3, 4, or 10 pints and cause not one bit of bother, finish their night out, and go home to bed...I never could.

Anyway my court date for the car offences soon came up, and I went to Chris`s work to have my last pint and say good bye to him and whoever else wanted to say good bye. We left with a hug and him wishing me all the best, and I left the pub knowing I would be in prison that evening.

As I left the pub an old Jersey lady said goodbye to me; we always greeted each other but further than that our conversation was very limited.

"Where's your friend going to?" She asked Chris when I had left. He told her the story and how I had no fixed abode and was certain to be jailed and perhaps even put off the Island.

Ten minutes later I'm standing in the court and the door opened and in came this lady, her name was Rose Brint. She sort of gave me a knowing nod when I said hello and we waited till the Centenier came into court.

At this point Mrs. Brint, Rose, handed me a small piece of paper with her address on it.

“Tell them you live with me and my family and at least you have a fixed abode” she whispered. I was awestruck. Why was she helping me when she didn’t even know me? I didn`t feel it time to ask and carried on with my downtrodden look for the Centenier.

“No fixed abode, eh?” He almost creamed.

“I actually do now have one, your honour.” I muttered handing over the piece of paper.

“We’ll need to get this checked and if you’re telling lies it’s going to be much worse for you James Joseph Toner”. At that point Rose stood up and asked to speak. She told the Judge that she knew me from the bar we used and that she was going to give me digs when I got out of jail. She showed some ID and he was happy with that.

He then read out the charges and the sentences.

“James Joseph Toner you have pled guilty to the charges led by the prosecutor, the charges and sentences are:”

(1) Taking and driving away, 3 weeks’ prison.

(2) Driving while under the influence of Alcohol or Drugs, 3 weeks' prison.

(3) Failing to stop and report an accident, 3 weeks' prison.

(4) Driving without a licence, 3 weeks in prison.

(5) Driving with no insurance, 3 weeks in prison.

(6) Various offences of entering vehicles not belonging to you, 3 weeks in Prison.

My arithmetic is good enough to know that I had just been given 18 weeks in jail and I was totally gutted. They took me out of the dock and through the back to the cells, but not before Centenier Le Broq had this to say. It is not verbatim because it happened so many years ago.

"We are here today to pass sentence on this young man who has come from Scotland to find work here in Jersey. He appears to be hard working enough, and has been spoken for by a lady of good standing here on Jersey. It appears to me that he was on a leaving night for one of his friends and they attended one of the increasing number of clubs on this island who are almost giving away the alcohol for free. That is the root cause of the problem here today. I shall be making a full report to the licensing committee for its thoughts on these drink till you fall down nights."

"Of course, James is responsible for his own actions and I think it is commendable that he has not wasted any of the courts time here today by pleading Not Guilty.

Unfortunately, the law dictates that anyone caught driving under the influence of drink or drugs here on Jersey is imprisoned and banned from driving any sort of vehicle."

And so I was sat through the back in the cells when the free Government lawyer came in and said well done, the Judge took to you there.

"Are you joking? He has just given me 18 weeks in jail, and that's him taking to me?" I couldn`t help but smile at that one.

The lawyer looked at me and said to me that I had only been given 3 weeks, all the other 3 weeks were to run concurrently with the drink driving one. "With good behaviour you will be out of La Moye jail in 2 weeks, ma boy." He said in his Jersey twang.

I was over the moon of course; my 18 weeks had just turned to 3, and if I kept out of bother only 2. Fuckin magic and I couldn`t believe it. I had to sit till the afternoon session was over, then the prisoners going to La Moye were all transported up together. I had not been in prison before, but nothing of note happened while I was in there except the first space shuttle crash, but that had fuck all to do with me.

So now I was seeing the progression of my alcohol allergy. It had now landed me in jail, and I still hadn't put 2 and 2 together. It was just me being me. Well anyone who knows anything at all about alcohol, and I don't mean drinking it, would know that's not how it happens. It gets much worse before it gets anywhere near getting better. I had the problem that some call alcoholism, and anyone who has that problem is an alcoholic, plain and simple.

Nothing of note happened during my 2 weeks in La Moye jail, but the 2 weeks' loss of my liberty made me value it a bit more I think. Two weeks later, and I'm out of La Moye and back in the pub. Common as fuck that is you know; someone gets the jail because of an alcohol related offence, and the first thing they do when they get out is get pished. That's what I did, and then headed along to see my new landlady with a big bunch of flowers as a gift to her for the way she had stood up for me.

Gradually my alcohol intake got worse and worse in Jersey but it wasn`t all shit tales of woe. Even some of the alcohol stories had their funny sides to them.

One of the funnier moments was when I had begun hanging about with these other Glasgow boys who I had met in the dancing on the Island. Joe Quinn, his brother James, and another lad called Steph. Steph was dark skinned so he'd been nicknamed Mowgli. One night it was Steph`s birthday, and we had scrambled the cash together to go out and celebrate the beginning of another year for him, and the rest of us too I suppose.

We had gone to this club, and I did this thing when I`d had enough and just vanished. Give me my coat, I'm going to the toilet sort of thing. So I had just headed home and gone to my bed. I woke up with the room in bedlam, cakes everywhere. I, in my drunken sleep, ate 2 muffins and fell back asleep.

I got up in the morning, and together with James Quinn we left to go to work. At the bottom of the guesthouse stairs was a baker's shop called Le Brun`s. The large plate window was being boarded up as we walked past, he smiled and I went ooft. We parted ways, and he went off to his graft in town and I went to mine on the other side of the Island. I was working with Eddie and Rab on the roofs, and it was December and fucking cold. I was on the roof and saw this wee Vauxhall Nova car pulling up. With hindsight it was definitely a police car, but I thought it was a car with people from the tax office or social security scanning the job. I ran round shouting and warning all my colleagues that it was on top and that it was best if they got to fuck.

Well the site soon emptied, with men scrambling down scaffolding and jumping out of the lower windows in to the snowy fields at the back of the building and making their escape. It felt good being able to help the lads get away from whoever these cunts were.

Then the agent came up the ladder and said, "Jimmy, the police are downstairs and want a word with you." Me? I`d done fuck all, in my eyes at least.

"Hello James." One of them addressed me.

“What can I do for you guys today then?” I replied in a mood of petulance. I`d done fuck all and they were at my work hassling me.

“Where were you last night between the hours of 11.30 and 1 o clock”?

“In my bed trying to get some kip for work.” I answered them back.

“Are you sure?” Said the one who was obviously going to be the prick.

“Where do you think I was then, officer”?

“We`d like you to accompany us to the station, Jock.” Said cheeky boy.

“Jock`s not nice mate, is it?”

Policemen for some reason don’t like being called mate, you’d think they`d be grateful for the people who would have them as friends.

“I`m not your fucking mate so don’t think I am, Jock.”

“Enough of the Jock then mate and we`ll be just fine.”

“Your colleague appears to be having no bother with me, why are you getting all stroppy”.

“I`m Scottish and you’re not my mate. I’m ok with that, but you still haven’t told me why I’m in the back of this police car and heading to your headquarters. What have I done?”

“There was a robbery at the Le Brun`s at the top of Bath street last night, and we have reason to believe that you were involved.”

“You mean you think I robbed the bakers?” I couldn`t help but laugh at that one.

“Is it because I’m fat you’ve pulled me in for this one”?

The other copper at this point asked me to calm down and let’s try get this sorted out. It could all be a misunderstanding, he said.

We drove through St Helier straight to James Quinn’s job, and the police went into the job and came back out with him too.

“What happening James?”

“Something about a heist at Le Bruns last night.” I said, while stifling the laughter I felt at the stupidity of it all.

“Don’t know anything about it.” He said. Stock answers the world round when asked a question by a policeman.

They took us both to the local police station and put us in a room with Joe and Mowgli. Wee Joe who was about 5 feet 4 was raging, and Mowgli had been shedding tears for sure.

“What the fuck is this Steph?”

“How did they find out where we all worked?”

“I told them.” He cried again.

Next thing the door opens and my name is called. I walk down the clean smelling corridor flanked by good cop and bad cop. We entered a room and they told me to sit down.

“Like a cigarette James?” Good cop asked.

“No thanks, I don’t smoke.”

“So Jock, tell us what happened last night at the baker’s shop?”

“Why the Jock pish, my boy?” I retorted in my best Jersey bean accent.

“You be careful with that lip of yours son or I’ll belt you one

“Well I’m not a Jock, I’m Scottish, and my mum and dad weren’t related till they got married.” I grinned back at them.

The bad cop was fucking fuming, but he knew I was in the right and that I had fuck all to do with the window going in and the cakes being stolen.

“Listen, I left the club early, went home and woke up to a tea party. I ate 2 muffins and went back to sleep.

At this point bad cop had an orgasm and he bounced around the room like he`d got Ronnie Biggs.

“Got you, Jock cunt” he sneered.

“And my mum and Dad aren’t Brother and Sister” I smiled back at him.

They both left the room and left me sitting for about 20 minutes.

“You’re free to go, James.” Said good cop.

“Big investigation done is it, officer?” I asked him.

“You can speak to your friends before you go.”

I went into the big room I had been in before, and looked at Mowgli once again. I could see he had been taking enough shit from his mates without me giving him any more grief. Wee Joe had put his hands up and admitted kicking in the window, and the other 2 had admitted stealing the cakes.

Not exactly the need for Sherlock Holmes on this one, because Hansel and Gretel could have followed the trail of cakes and crumbs to the room we all shared upstairs from the bakers and that would have been that.

I was allowed to go, and they spent one more night in jail before being fined in the court the next morning. Shame on them all for the Big Le Brun`s Heist of 1985.

One last wee Jersey story before I move on with my tale. I had been out drinking most of the day, and was on my way home I think. I saw this open topped car with a big old fashioned ghetto blaster in the back.

“Oi, get to fuck. That’s not your car, you cunt.” Said this big bloke.

“Is it yours like?” I asked him.

I didn't even see the kick coming, but I felt it crack the side of my head. I fell to the ground stunned, and he just walked away.

I got up rather dazed from the fly kick he had inflicted on the side of my brain.

"Ya big cunt ye, am half your size and that's the best you can do."

He came back and hit me 4 or 5 times on the face, he was sharp and I could do nothing to defend myself. When I hit the ground he walked away again, gentleman obviously.

I had taken enough so I decided to bottle the big cunt, into the nearest bin I went and very non-surreptitiously, I followed him making as much noise as I could, and warning him all the way what I was going to do with the bottle when I got him. We got down to the precinct and I made my move, charged him, and made the big mistake of throwing the bottle. It flew past him and hit a parked car, the big gentleman just put me in a head lock and asked if someone could call the Police, didn`t hit me once.

The Police were on the scene in minutes, and it was off to the cop shop for me again, another day spoiled by me being drunk but not getting it yet. Lack of power was my dilemma. I was released the next morning to appear, but before that could happen I received a call in the pub I drank in. It was the guy whose car I had hit; if I paid him £75 quid he would drop the part of the charge he was involved in. The big guy I had been battered off didn't even want to press charges, so all I had to do was pay the £75 and that would be the end of it. He`s still waiting on his money. I just couldn't give a fuck. £75 bought beer, and I`d take the consequences of that action when they came.

I have a million Jersey tales, but the book isn't about Jersey, so I`ll move on with fond memories of the wee Island in the Channel. I loved my time there although with the benefit of being able to look back that's when my drinking became "problematic".

I went back to Glasgow for the Christmas of 1986 and never returned to Jersey. That wasn`t the plan but I had gotten myself into enough sticky situations in the 2 years I was there. I`d have ended up a Sticky Bandit long before Beamer, Brown, and Allan formed the sticky bandits years later.

Chapter 4: Tickling the Underbelly

The end of the 1980s and my return from Jersey had a couple of effects on my life that I could not have foreseen, that said none of us can read the future or know what's going to happen next in life, or can we?

I came back from Jersey in December 1986, the plan was to maybe go back after Christmas, but you know what they say about the best laid plans and all that.

I met this girl, didn't really meet her as I'd known her for a long time, but we started seeing one another and spending a lot of time together. It was my first serious relationship. She was seventeen and I was twenty-one, nothing up with that but her family, especially her dad, was set against us being together, and eight months later he was proved right.

Donna worked and I didn't for a start; I'd had enough of work in Jersey for a while so I wasn`t planning on doing anything back home.

I had started to smoke hash and it became an everyday habit for me. I prided myself on the fact that I never once took tobacco. I was also drinking, but it was more of a weekend thing when me and Donna would go out for a few drinks in town. All very civilised at this point and the relationship was going fine. I thought I was in love but what I now know is I was discovering codependence.

Co-dependence turns to obsession and is very unhealthy in whatever form it manifests itself.

I had become dependent on our being with one another although we both did our own things with our own mates. It was the fact she was on my mind 24 hours a day and it was driving me mad. I hadn`t experienced this before but only because I hadn't been in a relationship before.

I was becoming involved in petty crime and began selling small bits of hash to keep my own wee "not a habit" going. Sure you can't get addicted to hash can you? The answer to that is it becomes something else that you are either using for your enjoyment or you are becoming codependent on that as well. I fell into the latter bracket.

So Donna had this proper job and I was buying and selling, mostly doing anything to keep me going and to make sure I had the money to go out at the weekend. I was in the rag trade (selling stolen gear) but mostly it was from selling small bits of hash that I made my money from. This didn`t sit too well with her dad who only had his lassie's wellbeing in mind.

So by the summer of 1987, not even a year since I'd returned from Jersey, I thought I was in love. I know now I liked her but love it was not. You don't behave the way I did if you love yourself and to love someone else you have to have a deep love of the person you are. Ah fuckin hated maself with a passion, so our thing was never going to work.

It all came to a head for me during the summer of 1987 and landed me in jail for the second time in my life, the first being a short three-week stint in Jersey`s La Moye Prison. This time it was to be Glasgow's notorious H.M.P Barlinnie that housed me for a couple of weeks. This time no half-joking drunken shenanigans, this time my jealousy, anger, and the fact I could be violent were to be the reason for my time in jail.

The relationship was going along just fine till Donna went on a holiday she had planned months before with her friends, before we got together as a couple.

I had lost control of a situation that I was manipulating but didn't even know it. She went to Greece and all I did was worry the full two weeks she was away. What if she meets someone else? What if she doesn`t want me when she comes back? I had a million "what if" questions and they all did my head right in. I allowed the fourteen days to feel like ten years in my head. Looking back, I was torturing myself and worrying about shit that I had no control over.

Donna came back from Greece on the Saturday so I didn't see her till the Sunday for a very short period of time. She told me about her holiday, I told her I wasn`t interested. She gave me the few presents she had bought for me and one of them was this litre bottle of Ouzo. Fantastic, but I was still to discover that I had this "allergy" to anything that had alcohol in it. Only thing was I didn`t come out in a rash, I became this sort of monster that people put up with at first but slowly and surely the monster became bigger than the joker and the clown.

The Monday after Donna came home she went to her work and I went along to my friend's house. Chris was the lad I went to Jersey with originally and he`d come home too, but he was to go back not long afterwards and has made a good life for himself there now with his wife Sandy.

Chris`s younger Brother John was there that day too and the three of us rattled the litre of Ouzo. I was paralytic drunk but John and Chris didn't seem to be as drunk as I was.

In my head I couldn't wait till the back of five because that's when Donna came off the bus from her work. I was totally incapable of any conversation or in fact as it turned out even civility. At 5 o clock I made my excuses and left to go to the end of the street to meet her from the bus. That wasn`t the best decision I made that day, nor in fact was it the worst as it turns out.

Donna got off the bus and had one look at me in the state I was in and walked straight past me.

"What's up with your face?" I snarled.

"Look at the state of you James, I don't want to speak to you in that state." she said as she kept walking on past me.

"I won't be seeing you tonight," she continued, "I'm going down to Langside College to enrol in a Higher English class."

“I`ve not seen you in two weeks and you’re going down to enrol in some stupid college course?” I said in drunken disbelief.

Her house was on the way to mine so I followed her to her close and she told me to go home and sleep my drunken state off and she`d see me the following day.

That just wasn’t good enough for me and I kept following her up the stairs to her house.

“Don’t think you are coming in here in that state, James.”

With those words, or words to that effect, she closed her door on me and left me standing outside her door. I went berserk, kicking and punching the door. All these defects I had in my character were now coming to the fore. The alcohol had blown my cover; I wasn’t just a clown; I was a madman as well. I punched in her door window and Donna came out to the stair landing.

Words were exchanged and I don’t know what was said, but in the end I hit her. I`m not sure exactly what I did, but I lifted my hands and hit the girl I was so sure I loved. She managed to get back into her house - which in hindsight was probably a Godsend - and I walked down her close and smashed the landing windows with my hands on the way. There will be those reading this in shock and thinking that I was some sort of freak, and that’s right, I was that day. I`m not boasting about this story, I’m trying to tell you all the way it was in the days when I drank. Think of me whatever you like, that's what people do anyway. Again, at this point in the story there may be some of you who are identifying with some of the words I have written. Good, alcohol might not be your friend either.

I just walked along the road to Bogany flats and hid in one of my friends' houses. I watched as the police went to Donnas house and then again as they went to my mum`s door. I hid while the police went through my mum`s house looking for me. Pretty shite is what I now think of that.

The police left my house and a short while later Martin, my wee brother, came out of the house and headed for the safe house I was hiding in. He was none too pleased to be honest, but told me that the officer in charge had told him that it wasn't that bad, and if I handed myself in that night I'd be bailed to appear again and they wouldn`t come back to my mum`s house looking for me there and pestering her.

So we both headed down to the station and I did one of the hardest things I had had to do till that point. Handing yourself into the police is not something we do naturally in Glasgow or I'm sure anywhere else in the world. Nowadays, I'm sure I'd add India to the top of that list. I walked in and told them my name. They were expecting me which was a bit weird, and I sat down to wait.

The officer in charge called me into his office and even allowed Martin to accompany me in for the interview. There was no interview; I was warned not to go near Donnas common close or her home and charged with assault, breach of peace, and malicious damage.

“Behave yourself James for fuck’s sake.” was all that the policeman said to me. “Now away you go and don’t let me see you back in here.”

I thanked him for not coming down hard on me, and with that we left the Police Station. Martin went one way down to his girlfriend Michelle’s house, and I went the other way back up to Bogany. As I got nearer Donnas house this thing that a lot of people like me who can’t handle drink came over me. I was going to go up to her door and say sorry; that should make things right was my reasoning behind those thoughts I now reckon. Anyway that was the worst decision of the day by far.

Up the stair I went and knocked the door, Donna opened it and looked like she had seen a ghost. Next thing her dad flew out of the sitting room and attacked me, quite rightly so I will add at this point. We rolled about on the stairs for a bit but it wasn`t really a fight, more of a wrestle than anything else then one of his friends broke it up. I carried a grievance against the guy who broke that fight up for a long time but he didn`t touch me, he stopped the fight. Without going into all the ins and outs of it, I ended up in Barlinnie after being remanded by the Sheriff in the lower district court for 5 weeks. That’s what I got for not listening and doing what I thought was the right thing. That’s not what I thought, I just couldn`t do normal things when drunk, it's as simple as that.

Today Donna and all her family speak to me, and are genuinely concerned about my well-being in my present situation. I`ve said my sorries and they have been accepted. It's another past experience.

Again, as in Jersey, nothing of note happened to me or round about me in Barlinnie, so I won't go into it except to say I was very frightened when I entered the place and was over the moon when I got out of it. It was, at that time, a big, decaying, and rancid old building. It did nothing though to prepare me for Mapusa JC or Vasco Sub jail Sada where I was to end up almost thirty years later.

Chapter 5: Not Big or Clever

My life of crime began when I was about twenty-one, I suppose when I came back from Jersey at Christmas of 1986. I began selling stolen clothing for someone very close to me who I'll call "The Squire". That isn't his real name of course, but this isn't one of those stories where I tell my story and involve everyone else in it. That`s still called grassing where I was brought up, and I could never be accused of being a grass.

The Squire was a few years younger than me but the head he had on his shoulders was so switched on to different ways of making money. He had grown up in a relatively poor house and had begun fending for himself, so to speak, from an early age. He had this job with a clothing company, and when he caught one of the drivers doing his turn and stealing some boxes of clothes he declared himself in. From the age of sixteen he was earning money in one day that grown men were working all week for, and when the driver got caught and didn't grass him, he had to find some other way of getting the gear out and sold.

I had just come back from Jersey, was skint, and we were very close as I have already said, so I was the outlet for him. He`d call me from his work and tell me that two "squiggles" were waiting for me outside the building. I`d dash across in a taxi, and in amongst the garbage would be two boxes with the squiggly line marked on them with a felt marker. They would be full of jeans, shirts, and t-shirts. I`d head up to Castlemilk and hit the pubs, of which there were two by now and the favourite was the Labour Club. In the "club", I`d sell as much as I could before he met me later that night after his work to split our share of the day's takings. I was always sitting waiting eagerly on him finishing his shift before we met and I got paid.

The Squire would do the tally up and give me my wages from the day's work, a percentage for picking the boxes up, and another share for knocking the gear out in the pubs, clubs, shops, and houses in the area. In the late 1980s, everyone in Castlemilk would have had something in their wardrobe they had bought from me or from The Squire himself. He was always hands on that way.

This continued maybe twice a week for long enough before he approached me with a proposition.

"How would you like to earn some real money James?"

"Sure I would." I replied. "What do you want me to do?"

He explained that he wanted me to do nothing but that he thought the money to be made was in selling hash. He suggested we put some money in together and begin a partnership selling the hash that everyone seemed to be smoking in the 1980s. This was the time when all you could hear coming out windows in Castlemilk would have been

Bob Marley, UB40, and the Glasgow band of the time, Scheme. I was right up for it.

I can't remember exact figures, but it was peanuts we put in together and bought an ounce of hash.

We cut it into smaller pieces and sold them on to other smokers who maybe didn't know where to look or were just afraid of the risk involved at the time in being caught with any drugs at all. Two days later, we went and bought our next bit and did the same thing with that. We kept the profit to allow the pot to grow, no pun intended there of course. Then the ounce became two, and we began to sell more of the product. It wasn't long before we had four ounces of hash that belonged to us, our own quarter pound. Hash dealers prided themselves in them days as to how much hash they actually had that was their own. Some had five kilos, some ten or twenty. We had our first QP, Quarter Pound.

But as was the way with me and money, I couldn't bear to think that some nights I had to stay in and we had hundreds of pounds lying there, and he wouldn`t allow me to touch any of it. He was in charge of the money. I used to sell the dope during the day when he was at his work in the clothing company, and he`d sell it at night time, so we had built up a wee network and I was about to cut my nose off to spite my face. Not for the first or last time in my life I was about to throw away my share of a going concern. A wee company that would grow and grow if we avoided the police who weren`t really on the ball at that time as far as the drugs squad went, and I was about to blow it for the sake of a night out.

I asked him for a sub out of the kitty, but he had planned to buy our first half pound - eight ounces - that week and needed the money at hand. I had the fever and had to get out on the town; it was the weekend and he wouldn't give me what was fairly mine. What difference would twenty-five quid make was my question. As we got older and grew up and got closer I was to find out. He always wanted to pay for whatever he "got", he didn't want to be working for anyone else, which is what you are effectively doing if you get hash on credit from them. He wanted his own half pound, our own, and I was trying to fuck it up was the way he saw it.

"Fuck you James, we're finished" he said to me as he gave me my initial outlay back together with a bonus. A bonus which didn't meet my requirements. "Are you having a fuckin laugh Squire?"

"No that`s what you're due, you took your money out so you don't get any fucking dividend, ya fat bastard". So we fought and punched lumps out of one another and I didn`t get out that night after all. I had been in a fight with someone who was younger and lighter, but he had the heart of a lion and I knew I'd been in a fight for sure. Don`t get me wrong, he would have as well, but that was me and the Squire not speaking, again not the first or last time, but it was awkward because we lived in close proximity to one another.

When we did see one another we ignored the other one, simple as that. Then I had no money and was missing the gift horse I'd punched in the mouth. I went to square things up with the Squire and we shook hands and put the fight behind us.

"What are you doing for money, James?"

"Not much, I'm pretty skint most of the time" I had to admit. He offered me the chance to sell some of his dope for him, work for him like I said before. I can`t remember the exact figures, but I ended up selling an ounce at a time for the Squire. I had to pay for the bit I'd taken before getting any more of it to sell to anyone else. In that lay a problem for me because I smoked dope and spent money. It didn't have to be mine, I spent the profit before it was profit, and that`s the way my drug dealing career pretty much went on for about fourteen years. Selling dope for someone smarter than me when it came to being wise with their money became a way of life for me.

The Squire and I fell out regularly, and it was during one of our fall outs that he heard I'd did a bit of "bag work" for someone else. Bag work is exactly what it says it is; you go and carry a bag to or from someone, and it usually contained drugs.

He approached me and asked me if I had done the wee job, picking up a bag of hash and delivering it to this other guy's customers. I told him I had and he was pretty pissed off at that. He had the same kind of work if I wanted it and it`d pay more, but I worked for him and no one else. I wasn't freelance, I worked for the Squire, and everyone who was involved in any way knew that. He paid me well and always looked out for me, never sent me anywhere he wouldn't have gone himself, and on the occasions that the hash was shite gear it was never my fault. A phone call and someone would come and collect it from him. This continued for some time in the late 1980s, and I always had something going on. Didn't work, played lots of golf, and to the outsider my life would have looked just great.

To an extent it was, but I was drinking and taking speed, and in a pretty volatile relationship at the time. So volatile that I thought nothing of lifting my hands, throwing things about, and smashing that woman's house up with no regard to the effect it had on her or her children. My life may have looked rosy on the surface, but lurking underneath were my demons of drink and drugs. I was yet to realise just how dangerous those demons were to my wellbeing and to my very sanity, but the day was coming when that realisation would slap me in the face.

Chapter 6: The Good Old Days

Then at the end of the 1980s, things just went mental. Ecstasy hit the Scottish streets, and the Squire had some contact that could get us some. Not many though at first; about twenty of these magic pills that everyone who had taken had absolutely loved. We were taking them in clubs that didn't play the right kind of music and didn't really have the kind of folk to be around when full of Ecstasy. Taking them in pubs and clubs and dancing like we had never danced before, but being in the tiny minority at the same time.

The tablets were expensive back then, £20 each but one did the trick, and you'd dance all night and meet loads of new friends, but they didn't get it because they weren`t on the wavelength that we were. Then Martin, my young brother, had the idea of running his own nights and getting everyone involved. Of course, this meant money being made from the pills. No one expected it to take off the way it did, but the late 80s and the early 90s were mad in terms of taking these pills and partying, then beginning to sell Ecstasy. Martin had the parties and The Squire provided the pills. Everyone was happy, because everyone was being paid a fair share.

The parties ranged from community halls beneath Bogany Flats to cellars in bars in town, and warehouses around the country to tents on the banks of Loch Lomond. If he wasn't putting a party on, Martin and his wife and all their friends, my friends too, would be through in Edinburgh or out in the town or at one of the club nights Martin put on in the Warehouse Nightclub in Glasgow. I was missing all this.

The nearest I got at first was selling the soft drinks at one of Martins parties at the bottom of Bogany Flats in 1990. Smoke machine, Desi D dancing and squeaking his feet and shouting its 1990, the one-year buzz. Proper Es and proper music and buses turning up from clubs in town closing for the night and hearing about this rave, all good fun until the inevitable happened.

During one of the nights one lad had taken too much, looked too hard at the strobe and then had a fit. I didn't know him at the time but he is my friend to this day. We didn't know what to do with him. He was lying convulsing on the floor and the doorman with baseball bat and giant Rottweiler was patrolling the small area. The usual shouts of throw him down the hill or leave him round the corner pervaded, but the lad came out of his fit just in time for Strathclyde's finest to bust the party and close it down. Apparently the buses coming from Ayr and the fact the egg boxes don't insulate a room from sound drew their attention and that was that.

Gradually, Bogany Hilton became notorious as the "block" at the end of Bogany Terrace. It and the rest of Bogany had become practically lawless. Delivery vans were robbed the moment the driver turned his back, swarms of youngsters would appear and the vans would be opened and emptied by the time the driver came back down the stair or the lift from the Hilton.

You could buy any drug you wanted in Bogany, I say any, but by this time heroin had faded away and it was during this time I became aware of the "inverted snobbery" that surrounded the drug taking and dealing "business".

Anyone who smoked cannabis looked down their noses at pill poppers, anyone "fortunate" enough to have been introduced to cocaine, or in fact any other drug looked down their noses at heroin users. To such an extent that heroin users were the only ones classed as junkies, and chased and battered at any turn round the wrong corner. It must have been, and I'm sure still is, not much fun battling heroin addiction.

But I was getting in tune with the music and knew I was missing out on a movement that would define the late 80s and the early part of the 1990s. It may have been that evening when Bogany Flats became the Bogany Hilton. A name that became synonymous with it till its eventual demolition in 1993.

As people moved out they left their keys with someone else, normally me, and the house became a party house, a stash for drugs and weapons that were beginning to be more and more a part of the culture. It was certainly the darker side of drugs culture, but by the early 1990s, guns were becoming more a part of the underbelly of the drug scene, a scene that was the underbelly of life itself. Some of the empty flats became the houses of people who had never stayed there, and with the use of stolen credit card numbers, the era of home delivery of household goods using credit cards had arrived in Bogany. The only problem being that none of the names on the doors actually belonged to any of the people who were all getting new TVs. A classic bit of fraud that went on for long enough.

It wasn't all dark for me though. Martin had a pirate radio station that he put on one night a week to advertise parties, club nights, or even record shops. We used the empty houses in the flats and alternated between the North of the City one week and the South the next. The National House Service (NHS) was a big part of the dance culture for lot of young folk in Glasgow at that time. It was all done pre-recorded on DAT digital recording. No talk, no bull shit, and big shouts out for anyone. It was only harmless music to the masses of people who had heard it or looked forward to hearing it. He had four DJs playing music on the station, two one week and two the next. The McDonald Brothers, Terry and Jason, known across Scotland as 'Pussypower', Little Nemo, and a local lad who went by the name of Asterix. The four of them also did most of the music at Martins parties, although Terry and Jason were the main lads. Martin and the Pussypower boys eventually had a falling out at some point, but Pussypower went on to put on some of the biggest nights in Scotland in the early 90s, including

Cajmere, Aphex Twin, Evil Eddie Richards, and Carl Craig. 27 years later and the boys are still going strong. Between them two and Martin, I had some of the best nights of my life. My life was ok at the time; most of the real issues had still to surface though.

Anyway the Department of Trade and Industry don't allow for pirate radio stations, and I think I'd be correct in saying that the NHS was the only one going in Glasgow at the time. The DTI made it their job to close the NHS down. As I said it was only music, no talk over or shouting out for gangs or swearing or anything like that. They caught the radio station twice with their tracking technology and closed it down and confiscated the equipment. The second time was the last time it was ever heard in the houses of Glasgow and down the Clyde valley again. Cunts I thought at the time, and my thoughts about that have never changed.

The Hilton became party central, and as they began to rehouse people in preparation for its demolition in 1993, parties were held in flats that had been knocked into one, and every night of the weekend -from Friday to Monday - you could be assured of a good party up the Hilton. I partied and I sold the pills at the parties, and that period was among the best times of my life. There was something happening all the time and I was always given a bag of pills to sell on to the dancers who just loved one another. By 1992 I was out of the relationship I had bound myself to and was having fun, real fun, in my life. Ecstasy was playing a big part in it, but I was out all the time and, looking back, they were the best years of my life.

In January 1993, I made my first of many trips to Goa with Martin and his by then wife, Michelle. We came for the Goa Trance and jungle raves and that's what we got. Four weeks of almost solid partying in the jungle, aided by "Acid Eric`s" acid punch or mushroom extract or the pills which were readily available at all the parties back then. You could take your pick of any one of two, three, or even four of these raves any night of the week. I fell in love with Goa in 1993, a love affair that would last over fifteen years, and which would end as messy as any of the rest of them but for a slightly different reason. I didn't allow the dysentery I caught that first year to put me off coming back; I was only annoyed that the illness confined me to bed and curtailed my party activities.

It was also around 1993 that my life took another twist and I was asked to go pick up The Squire from a train station near Glasgow. I did, and he got off the train carrying this bag and not looking too pleased. The bag contained 20,000 ecstasy pills, and he had just brought them up the road from London by train. Something had happened and he was forced to bring them himself. That wasn't a great idea, and we spoke about it on the way home to Glasgow.

"Come and see me tomorrow James and we can talk about this mess, could be some nice money in it for you". So the next morning I went to his house and we spoke about the

Ecstasy market. He spoke about Martin and the parties he could put on and he, The Squire, could get these pills by the tens of thousands. We`d corner the market and make a fortune he said.

He was getting the pills from some firm in London who charged him about 7 pounds a pill. He`d give me ten pence for everyone we got and he`d pay me for going up and down to London to collect them. We were talking thousands of pounds now and I was hooked. I started to think that if we did 2 a month at that price, I'd be earning £4000 plus whatever the wage was for going for them plus being given the first shout at any parties Martin would be having in conjunction with The Squire. This was all me projecting the fantasy of being able to make money and not fucking blow it. I had a co-pilot at these parties and in truth we were both shite at it. We just loved the pills and got out of our heads and had pockets full of cash just stuffed into them. We are still very close to this day, and he is one of the people from back home who hasn't forgotten me. He has settled down, like you are meant to do when you grow up, but I have fond memories of the Snowballs, Dennis the Menaces, Rhubarb and Custards, and Disco Biscuits we churned out to our fellow ravers back in the day.

Again, judge me if you so please, but I did what I did and I fully expected the consequences to be dire if caught. I did the crime and would have done the time if things hadn't panned out the way they did. Once again, me and The Squire had a fall out over money and he did what he had done the last time, paid me off. Gave me my severance pay and told me that he and I were finished yet again. I was very fortunate that I was one of the few people he could entirely trust, and I knew the full ins and outs of the London connection and all that went with it. I was no longer a partner but was still trusted enough to go and pick the pills up down in London.

Fair play to The Squire, because he always met me down there, and always went to meet someone to pick them up before giving them to me to bring back up the road. Too much hands on was the Squire.

I`d fly down with him, or take money down on the bus or train, and he`d go meet his man then I'd bring the gear back up the road for it to be distributed in hundreds or thousands around the country; The Squire had it well sussed.

Martin's parties were still swinging, and the rounds of clubs up and down the country were done. Dealers were selling The Squire's Es in Glasgow, Edinburgh, Ayrshire, and as far north as Aberdeen. The Aberdeen connection got busted, and the lot of them up there turned grasses. About 5 lads got between 5 and 8 years each, but none of the grasses knew where The Squire lived, only that he was from Glasgow. The High court in Aberdeen gave one of my friends 5 years on the word of young party goers who had turned to give evidence against him. He got caught with 10 Es at Aberdeen station, but in court half a dozen young Aberdeen lads stood up and said he had sold them grams of speed and other drugs in the past. I wonder if their kids know that now.

The 90s progressed, and with it came a change in the drug market in the UK. Cocaine became the big thing, and it changed the full scene. People were too paranoid to party anymore and the party scene definitely took a dent from it. People I had been selling Es to for years suddenly became policemen in my head; they were all out to get me and the atmosphere changed in my eyes.

I started taking cocaine on a regular basis and took less Es. Then, as was always going to be the case, as it had been in the States for years and London for a while too, the Cocaine began to be washed up and turned into freebase or crack, whatever you like to call it. I was given it one time by a friend and I could not believe the belt I got from it. I had found my drug of choice but could in no way afford to keep a crack habit on the go. I tried to play the old robbing Peter to pay Paul, but that only lasts for so long till things collapse around about you.

I was still doing bag work, but I had become very lacklustre in the effort I put into the job. One time I had been sent down to London to collect the pills. The Squire had gone leaving me in a guest house at Kings Cross, not nice I know but the nearest area to the train station. I had secreted the 20,000 pills in the wardrobe of the guest house and had decided to head out to the nearest pub to have a few pints. I ended up steaming drunk and staggered back to the guest house in Kings Cross.

When I got there I realised that I didn't know the name of the guest house and they all looked the same to me in my drunken state. I did know if I lost them and or got caught I'd be dead. The Squire would have killed me, of that there can be no doubt. I had no option other than to walk along that full street of guest houses and try the key in every door until one eventually sprung opened. I was very lucky that time because my need to get drunk had almost cost me my career as a bag man and my relationship with The Squire. I`d have got the nick for sure and got an 8 at least for having the pills in my bag in my room. The drink took me that close that time, but I didn't learn from much in those days though.

Another time the drink almost lost me a bag was when the Squire and I went down to London to buy 10,000 acid blotting papers. They were 70 pence each so I had £7000 in a bag and hit London in the morning and met the Squire. I had once again booked into a guest house at Kings Cross and the Squire and I had a few beers while we waited on this connection of his producing the papers and me taking them up the road to Glasgow for a decent profit. They were £5 each at the time, so work it out in your head. A £4.30 profit on each bit of paper, and we were the ones making the profit. Well no really me but The Squire and whoever.

The contact down there was at it, and me and the Squire ended up bladdered after drinking all day waiting on this deal happening. I can't really recall what exactly happened, but I went into a bar for the toilet and was hit a cracker in the ribs, my cheek more than likely got me the sore one. My ribs were broken for sure so the Squire told me to get back to the guest house and he`d see me back there.

I did just that and ended up back at the guest house at Kings Cross, I was well drunk by this point too. The guest house wasn't ensuite, so the toilet was on the landing and shared by the folk on that landing and the landing above. I put the bag down and went into the toilet for a pee, but when I came back out I went downstairs instead of up to my room where I'd left the bag. I was so drunk I didn't know what the fuck I'd done with it.

I made my way down to the reception and spoke to the person on duty.

"I have had my bag stolen from outside my room door and if I don't get it back there will be some bother in this place". I was screaming and shouting for the police to be called, the fucking police. I was down to do a drug deal and I thought I had the right to get the police involved in the return of my bag.

"I want every room in this place searched and I better get my bag back, get the police and get them quick".

So the next thing, The Squire appears and he looks at me in a sort of perplexed manner and asks what's up. I tell him I've put the bag down and some cunt has lifted it but not to worry I've called the police.

He couldn't believe what he was hearing, "the fuckin polis James, are you for real?"

I assured him I would get the money back but he was for getting out of there that minute when in walk the police.

"Are you Mr. Johnstone?" asked the policeman.

I told him I was and continued to make far too much noise about the situation for The Squire's liking. I knew this would be a bad fall out if I lost £7000 and I also knew that it was my fault. What a tit I was, and I was beginning to sober up with some sore ribs as well.

The policeman asked to take my details, and I told him I was an oilrig worker who was down to buy a car from a buyer who had placed an advert in the Motor Mart. He asked what I was doing staying in a shit hole like the one I was in if I had that kind of money and I pointed to the station across the road and told him it was the first place that I came to when I got off the train that morning.

He explained that there was no way he could get all the rooms in the guest house searched, and that it was going to have to be one I put down to experience. All of this is in earshot of The Squire who was not looking very happy at all.

Just at that point, this fellow comes walking down the stairs and says to me, “is this your bag sir?”

I grabbed the bag off him and looked inside it to see if the money was still in it and it was. All wrapped up in a carrier bag and on top of it two motor magazines with a couple of nice cars circled and phone numbers written down beside them. The guy with the bag went on to explain that the bag had been lying outside the room door all the time I had been arguing with the reception staff. I had walked down stairs after coming out of the toilet and my room was on the landing above. I was so pissed that I immediately thought the bag had been stolen and made my complaint.

The policeman asked to see what seven grand looked like and had a wee look at the cars I had circled out in the magazines. He advised me that it would not be a good idea staying in that hotel that night because my shouting had alerted everyone that I had £7000, and that was and still is a lot of money. He offered me, The Squire, and a pal of his, a wee lift along the road to a nicer part of London for me to get my head down and sober up.

And so we three got into the back of this police car and were driven from Kings Cross to Euston Station. I`m not sure of the name of that road but you’re only talking a 5-minute drive along it. The Squire did not say a word all the way, and we left the car with me thanking the police for the job they were doing and for taking me to the other hotel.

Meanwhile The Squire had received a call saying that the trips were nearby, and a car would come and meet us soon to drop them off just before I was going to get the train back to Glasgow as was the original plan. He went off round the corner and came back with this brown manila A4 envelope along with a packet of these Purple Aum Acid papers. We didn't have much to say, and I made my way inside to catch the last train back to Glasgow which would get me there in the morning.

The journey was murder because as the effect of the alcohol wore off my ribs were starting to hurt like hell. I tried lying down on the floor of the train, sitting up, and walking up and down, but they were broken and nothing was taking the pain away from me. I tried to sleep but couldn`t and every shudder of the train was making them feel even more painful. I was happy, well happier when we got back into Glasgow and I made my way back home.

The Squire was flying up that morning so I had a wee sleep or as best as I could before he called me and woke me up.

"How do they look?" he asked, meaning the acid papers.

I hadn't even looked, so I told him I'd call him back in five minutes. When I had looked into the open packet they looked fine, real blotting paper and all perforated, but when I looked into the envelope I knew something was wrong. "Something was rotten in Denmark" as Shakespeare would have put it perhaps. The paper was the real blotting paper but there were no perforations on the sheets. I called The Squire back and told him he should come and see them and come as quickly as he could. He came up to my house and we went into the kitchen because my girlfriend was in the house.

I told him I thought they looked wrong. I wasn't sure what, but there should have been perforations on them at least. The paper was right but I thought he`d been stung. He had been, not one drop of LSD was on any of the paper I had brought up from London on that train. I had fought tooth and nail to get that bag back because I knew I would be hammered for losing it, and he had just gone and given some Jamaican conman £7000 for fuck all, he wasn`t going to get that back.

The only number he had for the black guy was a landline, and when we got the address traced and The Squire did his homework, the cunt had pulled the stroke on six different people and fucked off back to Jamaica. There was no way The Squire could get the money back, and he had to suffer a loss that could easily have been mine.

So my life carried on that way, doing "wee turns" here and there, earning good money, and then blowing it all on drugs and drink. It went from bad to worse, my cocaine habit was forming and I loved Budweiser and cocaine. I always found trouble, and soon it was affecting my relationships, and in truth I was a total mess. In 1996, The Squire was sent to jail for something or other, and my source of income disappeared too, although the odd wee turn did come every now and again.

Also in 1996, I got into a relationship and before I know it I'm a father by the end of 1997. My son Martin was born on Christmas Eve that year, but it would take me another four years of fucking about and causing bother before I would begin to look at James and what made him tick.

I did try. I went to college and did a small course that was basically an introduction to the caring field, a general Introduction. I followed that by going to Coatbridge College and doing an HNC in Social care. I was put on placement in the Parkhead Psychiatric Hospital. The course was 2 days at college, 2 days' placement and one-day home study. I could do that.

My second week at the hospital was also to be my last. I went in to the ward and this old Staff Nurse came up to me and said in the totally condescending tone

"Hello, how are you today?"

I replied that I was fine.

"I know your face but I'm not sure what ward you are in" she said to me.

"I`m a Social Care student on placement here 2 days a week." I told her.

She burst into a sort of manic laugh at the end of which she turned to me and straight faced said:

“I thought you were one of the patients.”

She turned on her heels and walked away to do her duties.

I turned and walked the other way to the staff room, put my jacket on, and walked out the door of that hospital for the last time as a student. I would return some time later as a member of Glasgow social work department to interview a young lad who was smoking too much cannabis and suffering from drug induced psychosis. There would be a lot of water under the bridge before that day though.

That old bastard of a staff nurse had actually done me a big favour by her ignorance of who was on her ward doing college placement. The following day, I went back to the college and spoke to the course coordinator and told him of my quandary and the fact I was not going to spend a year in that environment. I didn’t want to be a psychiatric nurse or I’d have been doing a different course. He said he would try to find me another placement.

They couldn’t get me the placement I wanted, but through a friend, Jim Fay, I secured a work placement with a youth work project in Castlemilk. I loved it and was good at it too, but every now and again I’d do something outrageous and put everything I was attempting to achieve back to the very start.

I was involved in workshops with young men from the different areas of Castlemilk. I had been one of them, and they took to me in a different way from the other staff, most of them anyway. The project gave me some sessional work and I felt part of the team. I was trying to change but still holding on to a wee bit of the edge of the towel, and it had some pull on me.

In 1999, I left the sessional post after telling the project coordinator that I thought he wasn't really managing the project as such, just clocking on and clocking off and allowing the workers to dictate to him. There was no real management or direction coming from him at all. I was giving it my all, but not everyone could have said the same. He actually asked me to have a word with them. I was a sessional worker in the project doing 16 hours per week, and the project coordinator wanted me to speak to his staff about commitment and pass my concerns on to them.

I thought long and hard about writing that here, because this book isn't about who did what and who didn't do what. I left the sessional post and was told "off the record" that when another full time post was coming round, I would be given consideration for that job.

The project did receive lottery funding for the post I was spoken to about, a post I had even had input to when it came to the manager filling out the application for the lottery fund grant. The post was advertised, and when I applied I wasn't even given an interview. I went to speak to the project leader about it. It was all nice and calm, but I was told I didn't have enough experience or a relevant qualification. I had enough experience to take the marginalised young people away to Biggar or Callander for weekends, but when it came to it he didn't want me on his team and I know now that it was because I spoke my mind; he didn't need or want strong characters like me working under him.

Another person who I held and still do hold in the highest regard was part of the committee who refused me the interview, an interview was all that I had asked for and did in fact expect. He came to my house to see me about my anxiety about not even receiving an interview. He is one of the most honest and straight men I have ever known or will ever know. He didn't do himself justice that day with his "party line" answers. I still love that man with all my heart to this day though.

But really, the bottom line is that I would have fucked that job up because of my chaotic lifestyle, but I would rather have been told that than flannelled as I was with talk of a lack of experience or qualifications. I wasn't ready for it yet. That is as plain and simple as the nose on my face for me to see today, but in 1999 I didn't get it. I tried to add the project leader on Facebook recently so I could tell him he had done the right thing but should have been open and honest about it; he never was good at confrontation and he perhaps thought that was what I was after again. He declined my request at any rate.

1999-2001 were the worst 3 years of my life. By then I was fucked with the drink and drugs and trying to hide it from everyone. I was being pretty successful at that, but having to do things that could have brought years in jail in order to keep the habit going.

Anyway, in September 2000 my young brother Martin found out about my crack habit and it broke his heart. I had gone to Blackpool for a stag weekend which turned into a week, but deep down I knew I had been careless and would pay for it. Martin's keys and phone were in my house because he had been away to Spain on holiday. When he came back, he had gone to my house and found the debris of my last crack binge.

His big brother was just a fucked up junkie in his eyes, and that`s what I was I suppose if I'm being honest. Spending hundreds every day and not giving one fuck about the fact I had this wee boy, who although his mum didn't allow me to see him, was still my son. Martin finding out was a blessing in disguise I suppose, and it brought an end to my crack abusing, although I was still drinking and sniffing cocaine, which in those days was still cocaine and not some relative of the drug. To fund this, I was still working for The Squire and it was all becoming too much for me to handle. I couldn't sleep in peace at night for fear of the inevitable knock at the door. A knock that would have come from heavily protected men armed with a battering ram and a hydraulic jack.

It all came to a head for me on Sunday 25th of February in 2001. I was in the local Labour Party Social club and had been all day. I went into the big hall near the end of the night to see if there were any single women about the place. I made the worst mistake of my life and interrupted a game of bingo. I was asked to leave by this lady, I told her what I thought of her, and she called me some name. I threw the contents of a glass over her, and next thing I recall is this big 6ft 2in doorman punching into me and dragging me towards the door.

I remember biting him on the top of his leg to warn him to leave me alone, and him screaming and taking his watch off. He made this show of handing it to one of the committee of the club and went for me again. This time he got too close, and in the wrestle that followed he put his finger in my mouth to try ripping my mouth open. I bit his finger and didn't stop biting until I had the end of it detached from his hand and in my mouth. He fainted and I knew I'd won that fight; I left the Labour Club that night like I was some sort of hero.

I went to friends who lived nearby and he cleaned me up, my nose was broken for sure and my jaw was killing me. I realised later that was from me biting into his finger and not letting it go until it came away from the rest of it. I woke the next morning with that feeling I had woken with a million times before in my life, a knot in my stomach and a feeling of impending doom. 100% fear and loathing of myself. I was on this other friend's settee this time, and when he got up in the morning he just looked at me and went sort of "ooft".

I asked him what had happened, and although he wasn't present he told me what he knew about the night before. The doorman had been out of order and I'd just did that thing that boys from places like Glasgow do when some big guy is battering them; there were no rules and I had equalised his size with my teeth and left the club the victor. I left my pal Lee`s house and headed towards my own home but stopped on the way at the local shopping arcade. I met a friend and told him about the carry on and we walked round the shops thinking nothing of it. That`s when Martin appeared and smiled at my two big black eyes caused by the nose break.

He asked what had happened and when I told him he was livid, saying 'don't you think he`d have went to the police about that, you idiot. In the Labour Club, in front of two hundred witnesses, and on camera, and you're walking about like you don't give a fuck. To be honest, I didn't give a fuck about myself, so I couldn't really care any less about some big bully who could have easily thrown me down the stairs of the place and that would have been that.

He suggested I get myself out of the road for a wee while until he could find out if the police were involved and what exactly the damage was. The answer to that one was simple; I had bitten his finger off, swallowed it, and in the morning shat his wedding ring out before taking it to the pawn shop and getting £30 for it. Of course I hadn't swallowed his finger or his ring, but the Castlemilk rumour mill brought that story back to me, it was me who started it.

He got on the phone and found a bolthole for me down in the Gorbals area of the city; it was fucking hellish. I was up a block of flats that faced another block and the police were never away from this place, of course every time they came I thought they were coming for me so it was not a great week hiding down there. At the end of the week, Martin told me that the word was that the big doorman was going to sort me out himself and hadn`t called the police and told them who it was, although I'm sure he must have been asked at the hospital but kept his mouth shut.

I felt better already and headed home but not to my own house, back to my mammy`s. I was involved with a football team at the time, and the Saturday habit was the game then the pub to sort out lottery sales and talk football. I usually had Budweiser but that day ordered a shandy. I drank the top off it and put it aside. I could not face the thought of getting drunk again, not that night anyway. The following day, Martin came to visit me and told me it had to stop or we would be having a serious fall out, he was fed up having to tidy his big brother's mess, and more or less told me that if it happened again we would be finished. That almost broke my heart; my wee brother telling me that my drinking and the bother it got me into was getting too much for him. The Squire had been telling me the same for long enough too.

I lay in my bed and cried my eyes out. I'd had enough of it all, and to be told that by my brother was all too much for me. I couldn't see where the answer would come from, but just lay and cried and cried till I fell asleep. That was the Sunday, the 4th of March 2001. I knew what I had to do and I didn't do it without some trepidation.

Chapter 7: The Fellowship and My Second Chance

My mate Andy was a year sober at the time, and he went to AA so I called him up. The conversation went something like this.

"Hello Andy, its James."

"Jamesey Boy, what's happening?" He asked, with a sort of spring in his voice if you can imagine that.

I`m sniffling away on the other side of the line and I told him I need help, the sniffles turning to crying he could not have helped but hearing. He asked if it was the drink and that brought a smile to my face, and I told him yes it was. I was fed up feeling like I did and wanted to do something about it.

"I`ll be straight over."

We sat and we talked about his drinking and how AA had changed his life. He asked if I wanted to go to a meeting with him, and I said yes I did. He said he`d take me that night but I made an excuse, so he said the Monday was just as good. My excuse for the Monday was genuine in that I took the team training on a Monday and couldn't miss that. Tuesday's my group night, he told me, so you`ll be going to your first meeting on Tuesday night.

And so on Tuesday the 13th of March 2001, I went to my first meeting of Alcoholics Anonymous, and to this day over 12 years later I have not touched one drop of alcohol. I have AA and the guy who took me to my first meeting to thank for that.

I should at this point say that I no longer consider myself to be an alcoholic, but I do recognize that I cannot drink in any shape or form. I also still believe that one drink could be enough to set me back on the road that I was on until I stopped drinking. What I'm saying is that although I'm no longer sure about alcoholism being an illness, and no longer one for putting myself into wee different boxes with a label, I do still credit AA for the change in me, and for laying a foundation to what I was to begin to really believe in and put into practice years later. In short, Alcoholics Anonymous saved my life at that point and is part of the reason I am sitting here writing this story today. If any of you are worried about your drinking pattern or associated behaviour, then AA could be the place for you. I would say to anyone who is broken with the drink and wants to stop, try a meeting of Alcoholics Anonymous; it works for some and not for others. It isn't for people who need it but for those who want it, is what they say in AA.

I soon learned that if I wanted to do it right then no cocaine either and I had to go straight. Get a job, but what could I do after all these years doing nothing but wasting my life. I did it anyway, I left the "drug game or business", or whatever you want to call it and started on a government course for people like me who had been long term unemployed. It was murder working for £135 per week and having to pay rent from that, in fact it was impossible, so I was soon in arrears with my rent and had them on my case as well. That was my own fault because I just had to fill in the forms and it would have been all taken care of by the government grants that we were receiving for rent and such like.

I was straight and going straight, it felt Magick. I got to as many AA meetings as I could, and slowly but surely got better. The urge for a drink has never came across me since I stopped over 12 years ago, but I know I still have to be careful because it's inside me and just waiting on the chance to come out and cause mayhem once again. I take it a day at a time and keep it simple. Treat others the way I would expect to be treated, and when I'm wrong I admit that I`m in the wrong.

I plodded along on this government course learning IT skills which we were told would be needed in any job we did. In my case that turned out to be right; I had this agreement with the boss man Alan Brown, someone else I owe my change to. He allowed me to use the time in the office for job searching and I searched and searched.

I wanted to work with young lads who were in trouble or had been getting into some sort of bother or another. I had done some voluntary work before along with my part-time job doing detached street work with young people on the streets of Castlemilk, so that was my angle for getting into one of these jobs. I got word back for 2 interviews, one with The Archdiocese of Glasgow and the other with Glasgow social work Department. Both were based in young people's units, or "Homes" as they were called in our day.

The first interview with the church went well but I didn't get the job, I was very disappointed by that, but AA had taught me enough to help me get on. The next was with the social work department and it was this group interview thing. I was asked back for a second interview. At the interview the two senior social work staff made me feel very comfortable indeed. I thought I had the job, and waited every day for the post man to put the letter through my box offering me the job but it never came. I was gutted, then one day I got a letter from the SW department asking me to come in to the office to meet the lady in charge of Glasgow's children's units.

I arrived wearing a light blue shirt, and was ushered into an office where the bloke from the previous interview was sat with this lady. She told me her name, Leslie Moody, and he had already introduced himself so Leslie began to speak.

"Do you know why you're here James?" She asked. I smiled and told her I hoped it was to sign the contract.

"No James." She said returning my smile. "It's to speak about your previous convictions that you have declared on your application."

In those days the application form had this wee bit of about 2 lines which asked you to declare your previous convictions. I had to put on mine "please see attached sheet" and stapled an A4 sheet of paper to the back of it with the list of my previous convictions. I also put at the bottom of it that if any came back I hadn't declared, it was because they were so old, and I also put that I didn't deny any of them because I knew they were all alcohol related from the 1980s so I had nothing to fear about them.

She began to question me about my drinking and that almost threw me over the edge. My light blue shirt was soaking wet and I was about to leave the room. I didn't think she had any right asking me about that, although I had declared it on my application form, but she soon told me that the young people I would be working with exhibited the same behaviour, and she didn't think my length of sobriety was long enough for me to be sure I could deal with anything that went on without perhaps getting the angry head on or at the worst even going back on the drink myself. I told her I couldn't promise anything about my drinking, but I thought I was a natural for the job.

She looked at her colleague, his name was Ronnie but his second name escapes me, and said to me that Ronnie thought I was ideal for the job but as she was the big boss the buck stopped with her. This was a safeguard for the young people and me, and she told me that they would be happy to have me on board.

I left that room feeling on top of the world, I had a job. I had landed a real job. It was only 13 week contracts to begin with, but as my time went by in there I`d be given the chance to get a full time post. I told them both there and then that my working in residential units was a stepping stone to the job I wanted in the addictions field. I wanted to help young people with drink and or drug issues and I saw this as the way for me to get in to that.

And that was my introduction to Glasgow social work department.

I think I included this in my writing to show that it is possible for a man to change from the person I was, doing the things that I was up to, if the person wants to change. I did. I ended up doing a job that was designed to make sure young people didn't turn out like me; even writing that at this period in my life feels ever so surreal.

I added all the stuff about my drug use and involvement in dealing not to make myself look big or clever, as I know it does neither. I had good times using drugs during the early 1990s, and I had really bad times using them in the latter half of that decade and the first year of this millennium. Ecstasy didn't fuck me up, cocaine did. I never injected heroin but I loved the crack pipe, different ends of the spectrum but both dirty nasty bastards when they get their claws into you. The cocaine monkey on my back is more like a giant gorilla compared to the allergy to alcohol I carry with me. I write this because I want the young person who might read this to realise that there is more to life than selling and in fact taking drugs.

Drugs have destroyed my family, yet my earlier opinion of the fact that it's a matter of choice has not changed at all. Take them, sell them, but be prepared for the consequences of your own actions. If you are going to use, educate yourself on how to minimise the risks. There is no safe way of using drugs, but there are safer ways. Assess the risks, access the information, reduce the harm.

Chapter 8: The Key to Life

Things went well with Glasgow social work department, but situations will change again and again and that's exactly what happened with me.

As I have already said, I didn't know it at the time but my introduction to the spiritual path I now try to follow was first instilled in me at an AA meeting and at all the AA meetings I have ever attended. AA is about more than just stopping drinking. It's about a new way of life that is based on their spiritual programme of 12 steps. I didn't do the 12 Steps properly, but I don't drink and I attempt to live a more spiritual life.

I will go into that a wee bit later on, but what I had learned at AA was to help me during the most difficult period of my life so far, much worse than the crack years, and even this experience I am now going through had nothing on the bombshell that was going to hit the Toner family in 2004.

I was still flying in life, it was fantastic. I had the job I had told them all I was going to have, and I had achieved it in less than 2 and half years after getting sober and going straight.

I was good at my job, and could see myself climbing the ladder in social work to be in a position to have an even greater effect on the lives of the young people I worked with at the time. So ah thought. I got on well with all my colleagues and began to see where I was in relation to the rest of the Social Work department. I wasn't one for lifting a phone and calling an office upstairs, I got off my arse and went up to see who I was speaking with. We were discussing people's lives after all. I had settled in and was enjoying my new vocation, one I had chosen and one that people thought I had no chance of ever achieving. I showed them although that wasn't what it was about. I just felt a sort of calling that I should be doing that job given my own upbringing and drug related back ground.

In my personal life things were getting better too, I was back in love with the only girl I had ever loved at that point. Or was that just another obsession based on my co dependence? I like to think not although at one point it may have been.

I had changed and she could feel it. Her family could see it and I was back in her life, and this time I hoped it would be for good. Well we know what life is like and it wasn't to be forever like I had hoped, but I don't think that any of our upbringings had prepared us for the next experience in the journey we call life. It had a profound effect on both of us, and for long enough she was one of the few people I could speak to about it.

It was June 29th 2004, a Tuesday. I was in Liverpool for training for my job, not sure why Glasgow Drug Workers have to go to Liverpool for the specialist training that me and Denise Alan, my young person's co-worker at the time, went down to receive.

It had been our second trip down in two weeks, but on the Tuesday night in question I received a call from my brother Martin`s wife, Michelle.

"Hi James, is Martin with you?"

I explained that I was down in Liverpool and hadn't spoken to him since the previous Friday.

"What`s wrong?" I asked.

"There`s nothing wrong, just can't get a hold of him James". She replied.

I asked her to get Martin to call me when he came home that night. I never received that call.

The following morning, I called Michelle and she told me Martin hadn't come home that night and she still hadn't heard from him. I told her I'd be on the first train back to Glasgow that afternoon and be at her house as soon as I got home. That day dragged in and my mind went into overdrive. It definitely was not like Martin to stay out all night. I knew deep down inside that he was in some sort of bother or even danger.

It was after nine in the evening before I reached Glasgow Central train station. Linda was waiting on me and I asked her to drive to Martins house, telling her he hadn't been home all night and Michelle couldn't contact him. We drove in silence; Linda must have felt my feelings of dread and uncertainty because at that time we were very close.

My mum was at Michelle`s when we arrived, and she looked terrible and Michelle looked very worried. She told me that Martin went out the previous morning to go to a gym owned by an associate, I choose that word rather than friend for a reason. The word friend is used far too often in the wrong context these days I believe. As we grow and know who we are ourselves then that is when our friends in life become more evident to us and our inward thoughts. The cunt who owned that gym was never Martin Toner's friend

Michelle reported Martins disappearance to Strathclyde Police, who for one reason or another didn't take it seriously.

They looked in cupboards and in car boots at twelve at night as they thought we were telling them lies due to a court case Martin had pending. They believed he was hiding or had run away. I wish to fuck he had run away but he hadn't.

Two weeks of searching by me and his friends and associates and Martin was found dead in a field by a farmer out collecting bales of hay. He had been murdered. As this is a book about me, I don't plan to go into the ins and outs of his killing other than to say I allowed it to totally destroy me and everything I had worked so hard to build up in the previous three years. I couldn't control my mind and it led me into a dark dark place once again.

The only difference between this time and the last time I had been in the dark place was I had not chosen it this time. I was not running about with bags of drugs and taking copious amounts at the same time. I was working, had a good job, paying my taxes, was in a good relationship, and was loving life as it was.

Unless you have had a sibling taken away from you like this, there isn`t any way I could describe the feelings that I went through at the time, but I'm going to try nonetheless to draw a wee mental picture of the mayhem that it brought to my life.

When he was first declared missing I knew he was dead, call it intuition if you like and I do, but I knew that when we found him he wouldn't be alive. After Martin had been missing for 2 long weeks, an ex-friend of his and I drove all over the West of Scotland, or so it seemed at the time, asking questions and putting our own lives in jeopardy at the same time. I in particular went to meet people I shouldn`t have in places I shouldn`t have been in, but I had to find Martin.

As I have said, Martin was found by a farmer at his work on the 13th July 2004, a man named John Baxter. I still think about that man to this day, and when I eventually got the opportunity to meet him I thanked him for finding Martin and asked him how it had affected him. We spoke for a wee while and when I left him I felt better in myself for meeting him, but also felt for the man who went to his work and found a murdered body in his field.

So then began the police investigation into his death, and they were way out when it came to what they thought had happened. Any clues or solid bits of information they got came from me. I had asked all the questions that they wouldn`t have got the answers to, and they would have been going round in circles if I hadn`t told them all that I knew.

The press reports went from the sublime to the ridiculous, and we as his family had to endure all sorts of nonsense in the papers. He was a married man with two children and a mother, he had been murdered and left in a field; those are the facts of the story. But as we all know, the press like to add bits on from unnamed sources, so a lot of shit was written about Martin and his alleged involvement in an international cocaine smuggling ring and the fact he was due to face trial in relation to that smuggling ring.

Matters are made worse in Scotland because the Prosecutor Fiscal doesn't allow the body of a murdered person to be given back to his family straight away, so we had to wait for 18 weeks before we got Martin back to bury his remains. I can`t begin to imagine how my mother felt during this time, but it was a bad time for his close and extended family too.

The after effects of Martin Toner`s murder were felt all around Glasgow and further afield as well.

In November of 2004, we got Martins body back and laid it to rest. I remember looking round at the mourners and seeing people who I know shouldn't have been there. Associates who know more about his disappearance and subsequent murder than I do were there. I have a mental image of a man in black leather gloves standing with his wife. His eyes would not meet mine. That was not to be the last time I saw that man, and he never could make eye contact with me.

Two weeks after the funeral and twenty weeks after Martins murder, the police inquiry was ongoing and I decided it was time to go back to my work. I felt I had taken long enough off and had to get back to some sort of normality. A normality I am still struggling to get back to as I write this.

I returned to my post as a young person's Worker with Glasgow social work department and everyone couldn`t have been any nicer to me but I felt two things; One that I had this secret but it wasn`t a secret, everyone knew something really personal about me and I knew it was spoken about when I wasn`t present. The other reason was I had lost all empathy with the client group and in fact had actually picked up a serious dislike for the stereotypical "Glasgow Junkie".

I made a decision to leave social work and return to my old trade as a plumber. My dad`s brother Frank, my Uncle Frank, got me back in and helped me get back into the plumbing groove. I never thought I'd have seen the day when I was back in the plumbing game. I always hated it, but it was better than social work for me at that time.

Then just after the Christmas of 2005 it came with a bang. I had a nervous breakdown, not just depression but I actually wanted to die myself. Someone had murdered my wee brother and I was doing nothing about it. What kind of man was that? I knew who was involved to a degree, and I did nothing about it. I became the guy I didn't like, the man who drove all his loved ones away, and who thought that taking copious amounts of cocaine would make things better for me.

I built a wall and wore the badge, my wee brother was murdered and I felt that I could act in any way I so desired; that of course was wrong. I stopped talking to people and let my mind run crazy. I thought about revenge, getting a gun in Glasgow isn`t hard if you know where to look for it, and I knew where to find the man the police told me they believed killed Martin. Me and one of Martin`s friends had sat for long enough planning it, and it was going to be done in public on the steps of the High Court in Glasgow. That`s what it had done to me and his friends. The friend actually had a wee huff with me when I cancelled the job. It had hurt him badly as well, he wanted to do it himself but I told him no. I remember he accused me of playing God, but I told him I wouldn't be able to look at him the same way again and it would also ruin his life. I believe to this day he would have done it without hesitation. He turned out to be another cunt.

Like I said before, this is my story and not anyone else's, but the police treated me and my family and friends like we were scum. Both Martin and myself have criminal records, and to me the police treated his death like "one off the numbers". The only two police officers I will mention are DI John Heffron, who was in charge of the case, and a young detective called Dennis O Donnel. They treated me like a human being who had lost his brother and I responded in kind. I won't mention the police who called me and Martin's wife liars, who told me that I should feel guilty because I knew things about people but wouldn't tell them. They know who they are and I hold nothing against them. It was the way they went about their shite job day in day out and we meant nothing to any of them. That is a fact. Mair cunts.

So between dealing with the police and trying to come to terms with the loss of my brother, I lost the plot.

I had a couple of close friends who knew I was nearing the edge and tried to keep me from falling in, William and his missus Rachel were always there for me. Even when I acted like I couldn't give a fuck, they still did. Did they act above and beyond the call of duty? Yes, they did. Did they put up with a friend acting like he didn't know them and couldn't give a fuck for them by way of his selfish actions? Aye, they did that too.

Then there was a guy called Craig Sherry. I had only known him a short time through our job in social work. Craig didn't understand what was going on in my head and didn't know half of the shite I was getting up to, but he tried to help me get my life heading in the right direction again. Time and time again I fucked it up with my "badge wearing couldn't give a fuck feeling sorry for myself and self-medicating attitude". If it had been left to me, there would be no Lenzie Plumbing company in Glasgow now, it would have gone up in smoke. Definite good cunt.

There was Lee who was always there to listen and put the tea and toast on. Who came to India on holiday when I was in jail and visited me a couple of times. I will get to that wee story a bit later on.

There were others, but they came and went, and at the time I built up a lot of resentment against a lot of people who I would have called friends. Today I can see the bigger picture and feel nothing about it or them. I don't mean that to sound bitter because bitter I am not. I can now understand that people can only put up with so much negative behaviour and attitude from other people and then they have to do what is best for them. They have to take a step back and allow the negative person to continue with their life and not allow the contagious negativity to spread like the virus it is: a virus that continues to spread far and wide on the planet we call Earth today.

I moved in with the family of my girlfriend at the time, Linda. They were fantastic with me and although we sometimes had our moments, I still have a wee place in a drawer in my heart for Linda, her mum treated me like I was her own son. They kept me together when I was falling apart, although the strain and stress became too much for Linda and I and we split up. No one's fault, she was trying to deal with something that was totally foreign to her and I was not communicating with her. She didn`t know how I felt because I wouldn't tell her. The wall grew higher and higher and I withdrew into myself further and further.

Cocaine was my only friend for some of that time and my mood, and by now depression, got worse and worse. I woke up one morning after New Year of 2006 and decided I couldn't go out the door; I stopped working and gave a fuck about no one or anything. It was my wee brother, no one else's.

I wore the badge, the badge that gave me the right to do as I pleased even if that was to the detriment of anyone else, and it normally was.

So I thank Linda, her mum Margaret, her brother Craig and his Dad, Jim, and Big Buddy for keeping me going in my deepest darkest moments. (Margaret and Jim have both since died with cancer) both definitely good cunts. I wish I'd known then what I do now about that bastardin cancer.

I also have my love for football to thank too I suppose, my love for Castlemilk Dynamo the local amateur team kept me going and made sure I was ready for it every Sunday. I loved the boys in that team, although they may not have thought so at the time with my shouting and bawling at them at every turn, but they were another rock that I clung to for survival. It took my mind off things a lot more serious and kept me going.

They all know who they are, but again Nimmo, Worky, Big Willie, and a few others kept me alive. I continued with the football until the end of season 2007/08, the best season in Castlemilk Dynamo`s history. The year they won the Glasgow Sunday Amateur League and Cup before I led them out on to Almondvale, the home of Livingston Football Club for the Scottish Amateur Cup Final. May the 4th 2008 should have been my finest hour in my wee part time amateur football career, in one way it was and will be with me forever, but I was torn apart inside. The result didn't go our way but that would have made no difference to me. I had already made up my mind to come to India to travel, and perhaps to use the old cliché "to find myself", and that's what I did.

One of my oldest friends, and someone who had been in a bad position himself and more or less in the same position I was to find myself in, was at a bad stage in his life too and his mum asked me if I would take him along with me on my journey of discovery. To be perfectly honest I wanted to say no because I felt I needed to get away by myself, and thought the only way I could get better would have been to do that, but he had stood up for my brother and helped me out in the past so I agreed he could come along. I hope the time we spent together did help him overcome the shit that was going on in own life at the time, although I can't say for sure because we haven't had any contact in the past three years. Sometimes I wish I`d been bold enough to tell him no, but I felt sorry for him because he was more fucked than I was, and I felt partly responsible for that. He was doing some really horrible shit here, and in fact was heading for a serious mental breakdown or the jail. So ah wasn't fuckin selfish and told his ma he could come.

The 6 months we had in India were amazing; we started at the bottom and worked our way to the top. We saw things we had never seen before, jungle trips and Delhi, the Taj Mahal, and even went to the border with Pakistan where there is a daily closing of the border ceremony. Then we came down to Goa and chilled out for a few months before we went back home to Scotland. He was fit and had found himself a girlfriend, but I knew I couldn't live in Glasgow anymore, too many bad memories and too many people wanting to know what I was going to do about Martins death. I was trying to put that behind me and was succeeding. Glasgow would have drawn me back into all that "gangster shite" and I am no gangster.

I lasted 3 weeks before I knew that I had to come back here and get on a more spiritual path, a path that no one or anything external could have an effect on the way I felt. I also came to write a book, and when I look back at the stuff I was going to write in that, it would have been beside Reg McKay on the £2 rack within weeks. Perhaps being arrested was part of my destiny, maybe I just wasn't to write a book about who, where, and what concerning my past life and Martins murder, and maybe even being arrested here in India is a blessing in disguise. I don`t know.

I`m not sure about destiny and fate, I believe we are the masters of our own destiny because events that happens in our lives are generally caused by choices and decisions we have made ourselves, the way we feel about and act on them certainly is. But perhaps our final destiny has been decided but the road to it is all down to our own actions. I then counter that by thinking that if our destiny, final or not, is mapped out before we arrive at it then every single thought and action must be too.

And so then it was that I arrived back in Goa on the 24th April 2009, and was picked up at the airport by a very ex-friend called Tommo; he put me up for a few days before I got a nice little flat of my own in town. I felt freedom again, freedom from all that Glasgow meant to me. Of course I have friends and family back there but I hate the city and all its two bob gangster shite. If it wasn`t for my mother and my son, I wouldn't care if I never set foot in Glasgow ever again.

It was nearing the end of the season time here when I arrived, and was very quiet which suited me to a T. I did some sunbathing and messed around in general. 5 days before my arrest there was even a birthday party thrown for my 44th birthday. A nice wee quiet affair on the beach with cake and party hats, the lot.

And then 5 days later I was in Panjim Police station being told I was looking at ten years of my life being spent in Aguada Central Jail, a building on a cliff overlooking the Arabian sea, envisage Papillion if you can, as I can only imagine that Aguada - which is 500 years old - would be something like that

And that is the reason I found myself in India, my spiritual home which was soon to become part of my worst nightmare. I look back now at my time spent here and think not of time that has been wasted, but that it was like being at college or university. I have learned so much about life, about people in general, and more importantly about myself.

I carry no hate, not for the people who lured their friend, my brother to his death. Not for Omkar Mahalaxsmi, who will no doubt end up in a similar situation as mine as time passes and the political situation here in Goa changes. To carry hate about with you only brings you down, I found that out in the years following Martin's death. My heart is heavy no more, and I suppose in writing this book I am clearing the old shit out of my conscience that would hold me back for the rest of my life.

But all that is not the only reason I find myself here in India still today.

PART TWO

Chapter 9: Snatched

So I managed to get myself arrested in India on a cannabis charge, but mark my words; if I hadn't been sailing close to the wind I wouldn't have been caught up in the storm that is always sure to follow. To tell the truth about the actual events leading up to and my arrest, I have to take the story back a wee bit to the previous trip over there with my wee pal I told you about.

When we had arrived in India in 2008, we had limited funds but had a plan to buy some charas and send it back home to Scotland. We intended sending small pieces of hash back home in the hope that this would allow us to finance our 6-month sabbatical. We were a couple of fucked up cunts running away from ourselves remember, but we did just that and had some fucking party while we were doing so, and had some laughs and cried some along the way. Friends for life. Brothers in fact. Ha-ha.

I`ll not go into the ins and outs of it, but we managed to send some of it home successfully and that allowed us to go home with just as much in our pockets as we had gone over there with 6 months before. Hardly Howard Marks shit, but it was our wee turn. Well not actually ours because I'd only become aware of it when I was on the crack in 2007. Sitting in India with another fucked up crackhead from Glasgow who`d fallen out with another 2 fucked up crackheads (also from Glasgow) and couldn't tell me about their turn quick enough. As crackheads do, I fell out with the wee crackhead who had told me about the turn, and I then told the other 2 cunts that he`d ratted out on them. Can you see how fucked up and messy this all was? Not giving myself an easy life for sure. See if a crackhead doesn't get his/her breakfast and he/she believes that you owe them something, then it's a right shite mess in the post. The drugs definitely do that to you.

After that it was easy, and I just copied what he`d told me they did. Small potatoes, but enough to keep us over there in India running away from ourselves. After I returned to India in 2009, I thought I was clever and that I was only sending wee bits anyway. I kept sending the hash back, in cassette boxes or in daft boxes. Nothing elaborate or smart about my wee operation, but it was working and I was, on the face of it at least, happy. Was I fuck of course.

I had only been back in Goa a matter of weeks when someone asked me if I could source them a lump of the charas. It was more than I had been used to going up to Anjuna to get, but it would definitely have helped me fund my planned stay in India over the monsoon and beyond. If I`m honest, I thought I'd cracked it and started projecting forward and planning what I was going to do with the few bob I would make `the next time I got the dope for this other British guy`. Hadn't even been to get the first bit and I was already seeing this as my salvation, and I`d be able to stay out here forever. Well you really have to be careful what you wish for right enough, I almost was able to stay in the sun and away from all my real fucking responsibilities but it would have been in a bad place. Fuck.

And that's how I ended up heading to Anjuna to buy the 3 kilos of hash that would ultimately shape the direction of my life, and in that perverse back to front way it actually saved that life.

The day was Saturday the 23 May 2009, the time was 1 o'clock in the afternoon, and I was in the paradise that is Goa, India.

I was travelling in the front seat of a mini bus cum taxi cab which I had hired for the day to take me from my home in the South of Goa to the North side of the state. The driver didn't know it at the time, but we were going north to pick up a quantity of Charas. Charas is the Indian name for cannabis resin which I have smoked for the best part of 25 years, here in India and every other place I have visited on this planet we call Earth.

My routine was the same that day as it always was when I had to replenish my stock and, as I have already mentioned, help some friends out who didn't have the same contacts here in India that I had accumulated over the years.

This time I was going up to pick up 3 kilos that would cost roughly £2000. I stood to make about £500 for getting the dope for the lad, and it was a simple taxi journey there and back. Easy. While there I was also going to pick up 400 grams of some more expensive hash for me and a couple of boys from Colva; one hundred each for the two friends and the other two hundred for me. They would be paying through the nose for their stuff and I would be getting mine for free. You can call that free enterprise, you can see it as greed, but to me it was bread and butter. Supply and demand, they couldn't supply but did demand. It was all allowing me to hide from the real fucking world that I had no right hiding from.

The young lad I went to buy the Charas from that day I had known for years, his family even longer, but that counted for nothing that day. That was the day that friendships were lost. My tongue is firmly in my cheek as I write this of course. It all began the day before on the Friday when Omkar, his real name, called me to put my visit off till the following afternoon. I never really thought anything of it to be honest because I trusted him, Saturday would be just fine for me.

Omkar comes from a good family of old style Goans who had sold Charas to foreigners like me for 30 years. He broke the link because he got caught and began working for the police. More of that part of the story later though.

So it was that Saturday I went north in the taxi which was driven by the innocent driver, who unknown to him was about to get the fright of his life and all for the sake of £12.

I got to Omkar's place about 12.30 in the afternoon and he welcomed me into his home like he always did. I thought all was well and we spoke for a bit, had some soft drinks together, and then I left with the 3 kilos of commercial shitey hash in a bag and 400 grams of the finest Charas that money can buy in my pocket. That was me sorted for the upcoming monsoon season and it had not cost me one penny, for the season during which I had planned to try writing the book I spoke about earlier believe it or not. As I have already said, that book would have been bitter and full of shite about this and that, and not one I would have fancied reading myself most likely. I had come full of ideas of self-exposure and exposing the people I believed to be behind Martin's murder, and most of all to shit on Strathclyde Police for the part they played in it all. That was not how it was to turn out, thankfully.

So I left Omkar's house and got back in the taxi, not before telling Omkar that his "summer cold" was getting worse and he should stop it for a while. The summer cold being a reference to his constant sniffling that I immediately associated with one who was putting shite up their nose. "Not Cocaine" as it is now called in Glasgow.

"I`m cool James, my Russian girlfriend likes this so I take it with her."

I didn't look under the bed but I didn't see any sight of any Russian in the house. But what I did recognise at that moment, but didn't put it all together till much later, was a fucked up little coke freak telling lies. Takes one to know one perhaps you might already be thinking, and you would be right. With hindsight he was sniffling away, unable to make any sort of proper eye contact with me because he had sold me to the police, I`m hoping he sold me anyway and didn't just give me away to them for free. That would be a terrible dent to my EGO to think some little jungle rat had gifted a big, plump foreigner to his friends in the A.N.C (Anti-Narcotics Cell, the Goan equivalent of the drugs squad).

I was in and out of the little rat's house in no more than twenty minutes, twenty minutes in which he made the call to the A.N.C. He must have told the A.N.C that I would be coming past a certain spot at a certain time, because when I passed a certain spot not ten minutes later on the busy highway that Saturday afternoon, there they were. Waiting on me coming along to the ambush spot with my big haul of Charas were ten the finest Goan policemen you could have ever imagined.

I had at first felt some apprehension when I saw a police jeep pull out of a side street and settle about five cars behind me.

As it turns out they were not on my tail; my 'tail' was up ahead waiting on me.

The taxi approached the speed breaker on this busy highway at 1 o`clock in the afternoon, and as soon as we slowed down it all became apparent to me. Omkar had set me up with the police. No other explanation open to me, no one knew where I was going to that day except him. Little wank was the first thought to enter my mind, but in all honesty it all happened far too quickly for me even to have any substantial thoughts about what was happening. There would be plenty of time later to do all the thinking I desired. Everything around me went into a sort of tunnel, the sound became sharper and everything changed colour. I was in shock at that point in time I'm now sure. I felt as though I been lifted from my body and was looking down on the scene unfolding before me.

The hash was in a bag that had been sitting at my feet, and I just kicked it under the seat in the hope that they might not search the taxi. Silly that now knowing what I know about the cunts who arrested me. The other 400 grams of the fine stuff was in my pocket and came in the shape of Cadbury`s chocolate fingers, 40 of them, all 10 grams in each stick or finger. I knew I was in bother, but to be honest I didn't really think that the bother would be as severe as it eventually turned out to be. Money talks in Goa sure. Does it fuck unless you have millions of the stuff.

In a flash I had been thrown into the back of the taxi and was hastily driven away by the policeman who had taken the driver's place by this point. I wanted to kill that little fuck Mahalaxsmi at that moment, sometimes even now some three years later I still do, but only for a fleeting second does his little rat shaped face come into my mind, and I chase it back out again quicker than it appeared. He is Hindu, so will have a strong belief in Karma; my own thoughts on it are much simpler than the cycle of reincarnation. If you do bad shit to people in your life, then there is always a chance that something bad will happen back to you. Call it simple man`s Karma if you like.

I was driven to the local city of Panjim, which was about ten minutes away from the scene of the snatch, because that's what it was, a snatch. In Panjim I was taken to the headquarters of the A.N.C, the elite of Goa`s drug squad, and left sitting in an office in 100-degree heat without even a fan for any sort of comfort from temperatures which could have killed me. They went on about their business like I wasn't there at all, just the odd mention of foreigner and Charas, but not much else at all.

I asked to speak to the boss; he came along and told me his boss would be here soon enough. No problem, they would fix my case for me.

I smiled, they brought me water.

"Not long now James Toner." They knew my name.

"How long is not long Bhayia?" I asked.

"You speak Hindi James Toner?" They asked in English.

"May Torra torra Hindi Bolta hai." I told them, explaining 'yes but very little.'

I suppose I might have thought that would have helped me out of the 'wee mess' as I still thought it was at that point, but I was so far from being right in that respect. I was about to receive the biggest kick in the balls in a lifetime of severe ball kicking.

I was moved along the corridor after around 3 or 4 hours and taken into what I will attempt to describe to you all. I didn't know it at the time, but this dungeon would be my home for the following 7 days. Not that long I hear you say, no not really I suppose, I'd retort.

The cell was quite spacious, about 8 feet by 6 with the concrete slab that most jail cells in police stations have on the floor. Gives you the impression you're on a bed I suppose. It has never fooled me though.

I sat on the concrete slab and surveyed my surroundings as you do when you're in the dentist or doctors or any other waiting room. Waiting room this was not.

There was a small window about 6 feet from the ground which faced out into the courtyard of the police station, I didn't know at the time but this was the main police station in Goa. To be honest, at that time of the day in the month of May it afforded very little light and even less in the way of fresh air, but it was a window and that was a bonus in itself. It must have been around 6 o`clock, because it was getting dark and the mosquitoes were coming out in force in the room that was to be home for me and all my crazy thoughts over the next week.

The cell gate opened and there stood the head honcho, the investigating officer in my case. I`ll call him the I.O. His name is Punaji Gawas. His rank at that time was Police Sub Inspector, and next step up is Police Inspector itself. Stood beside him was this other Indian I had not seen at the scene of the snatch. Turns out he was the big boss, his name was Ashish Shirodkar, and his rank was that of Police Inspector.

He stood in the open door way and beckoned me out into the small corridor that led to the courtyard. I thought he wanted to talk money and freedom but I was not prepared for what happened next.

Gawas is a gormless looking cunt and always has this daft fucking smile on his face. I had the pleasure of telling him in the months to come what a wank I thought he was, and that I hoped his God looked after him in this and the rest of his lives. That frightens the Hindus and this guy knew he was, remember that.

They, accompanied by one of their goons, walked me along the outside of the courtyard to the A.N.C office and sat me down on a seat in the corner of the room.

"Relax James Toner." He said.

It can get right on your nerves when some swine is calling you by your full name and you don't know his, and even more so when you know he`s just about to put the hammer on you so to speak.

"How much is this going to cost me, boss?"

He smiled that smile I had already grown to hate and said the real boss was on his way. Hurry the fuck up then will you ya cunt, was all I could think at the time.

Then in walks this smarmy looking fuck with a grin from ear to ear. Turns out he is the boss`s boss, Police Inspector (P.I) Ashish Shirodkar. About my height or a bit bigger, but with the swagger that must come from either not wiping your arse right or the job the cunt was doing.

"James Toner."

"Yes sir." I replied.

"You are in very big trouble, this time." he said.

His sneer was confounded by the fact that he had a hair lip and maybe sneering was all he could do anyway.

“Sir, I have made a mistake and I know that I am at your mercy, how much will this mess cost to fix?”

“Yes, yes. Big mistake you have made James Toner. Ten years in Fort Aguada for you. You foreigners think you can come here and make business and not pay the police. You will find out now how we treat people like you who are spoiling our lovely, beautiful land”.

“Business sir? What do you mean business? I have 400 grams of Charas and that is not commercial quantity according to the laws of Goa and India sir”.

He then produced a white carrier bag from a drawer in the desk in front of him and said to me:

“This is your bag is it not, James Toner?”

“No sir, it is not my bag, I have never seen that bag before in my life.”

They all laughed at that one, but I was struggling to make sense of what was happening and definitely had lost that part of my character called ‘sense of humour’ by that point.

He ripped the bag open, and inside was a large quantity of Charas, old shit that had been hidden some place or even buried by the looks of it to me.

“What the fuck is that?” I demanded.

"Using bad words now, James Toner." PI Ashish Shirodkar said to me. I could only look at him aghast. I knew there was something wrong happening here, and I knew it was looking like I was on a hiding to nothing with these cunts.

"Don't worry James Toner, we can fix this mess and you can go back to England where you belong."

"I`m not from England, I'm from Scotland."

"I can fix your problem for you, James Toner, but it will cost you some money."

"How much money?" I asked, in more than a little bit of shock by this time.

"You have 2.75 Kilos of Charas in the bag so you will be going to Aguada for ten years, won't see your family for ten years, no jiggy jiggy for ten years."

"Fuck off ya cunt, I had 400 grams of Charas not 2.75 kilos of shite, a thought it was 3 kilos of shite, I want to see a lawyer and now."

The policemen present all had some laugh at the thought of me telling them I wanted to see a lawyer and that I wanted one now, I'd get to see a lawyer when they had made up their tale and not before. It would be the Monday before I did get the opportunity to speak to someone from the firm that was eventually to represent me in my fight.

They took me back along to the cell that I had been in before and as he closed the gate behind me, Shirodkar said to me, "$10,000 or its ten years for you."

I leaned closer to the bars on the gate and told him to fuck himself and to make sure that Omkar Mahalaxsmi knew I was going to kill him when I first got the chance to.

"Are you threatening me?" He asked.

"No, but I will kill that little fuck that gave me to you ya hair lipped fuckin bawbag." One of the things about speaking Glaswegian the way it's normally spoken at speed is that he didn't get much or indeed any of what I was saying to him. With that, he turned and left the corridor he was standing in, leaving me to look around the cell which I then knew I was going to sleep in that night. I was not given a blanket or mattress or even a pillow, this was India and you don't get that in an Indian police station. Or even in an Indian prison, as I would soon discover in the weeks and months ahead.

During my time along in the office, the cell had gained a couple of new lodgers who just stared at the foreigner, not really knowing what my reaction to them was going to be at all.

"Hello." I managed.

One of them was quite young and the other lad was older than me (at that point I was 44). They both looked like poor souls, and as the week progressed I got to know them both a bit better, and they were indeed poor wee souls. So was I at that particular moment in my life though, just a poor lost soul.

It must have been around 8 that first night when 5 Policemen came to take me to search my house in Colva. They walked me along to their office, where we sat for about fifteen minutes before someone gave the nod for us to head out to the waiting jeep.

As we got to the office door, I was pushed to the front of the group by one of the policemen and did not expect to walk straight into a barrage of flashbulbs and TV cameras. I was livid, shouting and bawling and cursing them upside down. I tried to pull my t-shirt over my head and fell over my own feet. I picked up one of my flip flops and threw it at the media scrum. That is what it was, a total melee of camera men attempting to get a shot of the foreigner who had been "caught" with drugs. I did not want this coverage to hit the UK news before I had the chance to speak to my mother about it; that's how I now explain my behaviour at that point in time.

I was bundled into the jeep and the policemen all piled in at my back, and drove the 40 or so km down to my flat where I knew they would find nothing anyway, but I was more than a bit concerned that they could perhaps add to the contents of the carrier bag after I had abused the top man in their office in Panjim. I thought maybe chemicals of some sort and then I'd most definitely fucked.

The journey down to my place took about an hour, and once we got there the dirty bastards were like kids a sweetie shop when they got to the apartment. Having found or indeed planted no further contraband in my flat, they proceeded to empty the contents of my wardrobe and fridge and then my bar. They were having a fucking party in my apartment and were even bouncing up and down on my big comfortable bed like they were all 3-year-olds again. Having found nothing of note, they were happy to head back into the jeep and take the leisurely drive back to their office. On the way we stopped at the local hospital for me to have a medical that would confirm that I was fit to be kept in the custody of the A.N.C in the dungeon that I was being taken back to. Joke in itself that is.

Once back in the police station they fed me with the usual Indian fare of dahl, rice, and chapatti. It was fuckin murder eating with my fingers in front of theses monkeys. I make no apologies for the use of the term monkey, I am not being racist. They were just acting like monkeys, plain and simple. I didn't eat much and asked where I'd be sleeping that night. 'In your room' one of them replied. I had taken a particular dislike to this fat bastard, and I didn't try to hide my contempt for him one little bit.

"Wank." I said smiling.

He smiled back, perhaps thinking I had thanked him in my Scottish tongue.

"Naw mate, you are a fuckin wank." I said right into his fat face.

They knew the word fucking of course, and they don't like being sworn at. But I don't particularly like being fucked over by anyone, and particularly by these bent Indian coppers. At this point in my tale I knew they were bent but didn't know the full extent of their corruption.

So I was taken back along the corridor to the cell that I was to be sleeping in that evening, the same one as before.

"In the corner, Puklha." He said.

"My name is James Toner, not fucking Puklha". Puklha is the Goan equivalent of the N word for us white skinned devils that were fucking up their idyllic paradise.

He marched away to his wee hard wooden seat that he managed to sleep on at every opportunity, and I turned to look for my bedding in the corner.

In the corner was a small pile of newspapers that had been lying for goodness knows how long, yellow and dirty. The two local prisoners looked at me and told me that was my bedding. One sheet to lie on and a couple more to cover me up and to use as sheets. For fuck's sake I thought.

I sat down and finally began to take in the vile surroundings that I had found myself in. I was not prepared for this in any way at all. I like my comforts, well I did till that point, and there appeared to be none in this establishment. The floor was filthy and covered in cigarette ends, discarded food, and the worst of all was this red shit that Indians chew, Tombacco. It is more or less guaranteed to give him or her cancer, but it is a cheap hit for them and it's their bag. Anyway, when they chew it they spit the residue wherever they stand, and the floor of this cell was covered with this red, bloodlike spittle. Dirty bastards, I thought, but that was just the start of my look about the cell.

One corner in particular was covered in this spit all the way up the wall, and that was complemented by blood stains and shite stains covering the full corner too, actual shite. Fuck knows what had been going on in that place, but it definitely hadn't been cleaned for many a year. I`d get the place cleaned in the morning I mused, ha fuckin ha. Some chance of that.

At the far end of the cell away from the gate were the 'toilet facilities'. For heaven's sake, I could not believe this at all. It was just like nothing I had ever seen in my entire life. I am a plumber remember, and I have been in some shitty situations, but this was like nothing I had ever experienced in my life. Then a remembered that ah had in a guy's house in the east end of Glasgow. I had gone on a home visit with a co-worker, big Paul Dowdalls. This house was being stripped and fumigated because the client - who had a serious drink and associated mental health problems - had been smearing his shite all over every single wall in that house. Anyway, that was Glasgow and this was not.

The toilet was split into three parts, one for doing the toilet, one for washing your hands and face, and the other which was the sort of shower room. The toilet was a hole in the ground, and again it was covered in shit all over the hole and all up the fucking walls as well. Dirty protests all round by the look of things. I wasn't looking forward to using this for a piss or a shit, but I knew it had to come at some point.

The other part that contained the wash hand basin was equally as filthy, and it was the same old story as before, shite and blood up all the walls and all over the basin too. The nearest I had ever come to seeing anything like this would have been in Trainspotting the movie. Renton in the toilet in the bookies and he drops his suppositories down the pan. I`m sure Irvine Welsh describes it better than I can in his book, but it was fuckin horrendous to say the least.

Having said that, if I'd dropped a lump of Charas down there at that point I think I'd have been down and got it like a shot as well. You are not allowed footwear in the cell, so it was bare feet for me too, and I suppose I should also add that I was plodding about in a couple of inches of piss, shite, and fuck knows what else.

I didn't expect the "shower" area to be any better I suppose, but I wasn't expecting the same blood and shit to be on the shower walls as well. Well it was. The actual shower was just a tap about 3 feet up the wall, and a bucket and jug was the method of getting washed. I didn't bother that night at all.

I went back into the main cell after my wee exploratory look at the facilities, and sat back down on the concrete slab that was a pseudo mattress, and looked at the other two who were staring straight back at me.

"Hello" said I.

The younger one acknowledged me but the older of the two didn't say anything at all.

"He doesn't speak English sir, but his name is Raj. My name is Ashish."

There is a subtle irony in the name if you look for it.

Then followed the usual jail shite about why we were there and the fact that Ashish was innocent of a bogus bouncing cheque case and the other fellow was a poor farmer who was having trouble with a builder. The builder beat him with a stick and he crowned him with a shovel. No denial on the part of the older bloke. He was being bullied and fought back, but in India it's the money that talks and the bullshit that walks. I saw the poor old guy crying a couple of times in the next few days because he just didn't have the money to fight his corner.

"What is your case then?" asks the young fella.

This was not my first taste of prison, so I played the game with him.

"I killed a cow on my bike".

"What?"

"A cow, a big fat slag sitting on my bike, so I hit her with Raj`s shovel and she fell down a big big hole".

Of course the cow is holy in these parts and he didn't quite get my nervous Glasgow sense of humour.

Smiling, I then told him my case was a Charas case but they were making it into a big story and I didn't really know what the charge would be.

"Don't worry Puklha, they don't like putting foreigners in jail here in Goa, in case one of you should die." He said, laughing.

"Listen son, my name is James and not fuckin Puklha or whatever you call me."

"It means white man or pale skin, and is not an offence Uncle." He said. Uncle is a term of respect that Indians give to people older than them.

"That's cool then, but I'd rather you called me James because that is my name."

With that, we three settled down and tried to get some sleep. It was virtually impossible for me to sleep that night because of the concrete slab, the used newspapers that were to be used as a sheet and mattress as well, and the smell of piss and shit that was impossible to hide from in the small hot cell. But the worst thing of all that stopped me getting any sleep at all were the mosquitoes that arrived in squadrons just as the sun was setting. There was no respite from these little fuckers all night, and the constant attacks didn't become any less in frequency or intensity until the morning when the sun came up once more and the mosquitoes went to sleep on the walls of the cell.

Add to that the racing mind of someone who knows he`s in bother of his own making, but doesn't know what the fuck is going on behind the language he doesn't understand.

Was I worried? You better believe I was worried. I believe it was the fear of the unknown that was concerning me more than the fear of being sent to prison and the loss of my freedom at that point. Later, I would still my mind again and try to make sense of all this, but it wasn't going to happen in that dungeon cell in Panjim police station.

The morning began with some lad from a local hotel coming into the jail with the 'breakfast'. Not the same breakfast that wee Benny or Jim or the Muir would have been bringing me back in the day, but two fuckin bread rolls and a cup of the sugariest tea you are ever likely to have tasted in your tea drinking life. I drank neither the tea nor ate the bread rolls. I would rather have fuckin starved if truth be told. But I wasn't starving, weans in fucking Africa and India are starving, ah was just going to be a wee bit hungry after. I had to settle my mind and attempt to make some sense of all this.

Later in the morning a couple of the ANC staff came to the cell to collect me and took me along to their office. It was airier, and although I entered with some trepidation it was like being out of jail, although I knew it was far from being out of jail. As I entered the office I glanced down and saw one of the Sunday papers lying with the headline about the foreigner caught with Charas. I picked it up and began to read the story.

'Acting on specific and reliable information the ANC had been lying in wait at Chapora Bus Stand with the knowledge that one foreigner would be coming at 3.30 with drugs to sell to a client that he would meet.'

“What the fuck is this shite all about?” I demanded to know.

Gawas, the I.O said to me, “It is a story that someone had given the papers and didn’t come from the police.”

My thoughts were immediately in turmoil again. If that were true, where is the client? Why have they made this up and why is there no mention of the taxi I was arrested in. I couldn’t understand how any newspaper would get their story so mixed up and far from the truth.

“Don’t worry James Toner, it is all a big mistake made by the newspapers.” Gawas said to me.

That gave me little or no comfort at all.

Later that day I was driven back down to a town near Colva called Margoa. It was a Sunday and the magistrate looked irate as he asked me if I had any complaints against the police. I felt the grip of the coppers hand at that point and just shook my head. In the words of the common scheme living Glasgow boy, “I shat myself” to open my mouth and tell this angry looking official that I had only a small bit but they said it was a bigger bit. That, and at that time I was admitting to nothing in any case.

During the drive back to Panjim, one of the officers asked me to turn my head the other way.

“Why, what`s the problem?” I asked of him.

"I don't like the way you are always smiling, James Toner." came his reply.

My smile grew wider at that and I kept aiming it in his direction, he had told me it was annoying him and that suited me to a T. He went on tell me I was not acting like any other foreigner he had ever arrested; they all struggled and most of them cried like big babies were his words.

I know now that although my mind was in turmoil, somewhere deep down inside me I had surrendered and accepted that this was to be my lot at that moment. My mind kept telling me different though.

It was a Sunday, and I didn`t know what to expect other than lie here till I was formally interviewed then charged. I should point out that at no time in the week when I was in the office was I formally interviewed or asked about the source of the drugs they had caught me with. I wonder why that was, eh?

Well the simple answer to that is that I had bought the Charas from Omkar Mahalaxsmi in Anjuna/ Vagator, but he was directly selling the cannabis for the police. I had fallen for a very simple sting that would not be exposed for another eight or nine months, but it would be exposed eventually.

At that point I held out some hope, but feared the worst to be honest. The following week in that police cell was the most horrid and at times surreal experience of my life.

On the Monday morning I was visited by the representatives of the British Government here in Goa. They are actually the British Tourist Assistance office, but the staff has titles such as Consul, Vice Consul, and Assistant Vice Consul.

That morning I met Karen Almedia, Vice Consul, and Andy Carvalho, Assistant Vice Consul. They explained that they couldn't help with legal matters but just wanted to make sure I was ok. They gave me a wee party pack with soap, toothpaste, and a toothbrush in it. I asked if I could use one of their phones to call my mum in Scotland, I was dreading this because I knew she was already shattered by Martins murder, and all she really needed to hear was that I had been arrested in India on a drug charge. At that point in time I still hadn't been informed of the actual charge as such. It would have been about half seven in the morning in Scotland, and the conversation went something like this.

"Hello Mum, how are you? Sorry for waking you up."

"That's ok James, what's wrong?" Replied my mother who knew something was not right.

"Right, I don't want you to panic but I've been arrested here in Goa with some hash on me."

I could hear the gasp of her breath, and could hear the sound of her beginning to cry. It was also me who had broken the news of Martin's murder to my mum, and I know how much that did and still does affect her.

"I want you to tell a couple of my friends and then get someone to come and sit with you for a while mum, don't sit all alone and worry about me. I will be ok; you know in the end I always am."

Thing is, it's one of your mammy`s jobs to worry about you, and most of them do so until the day they die. I know I have given my mum more cause to worry than most over the years and at that moment, and even now as I write this, if I have one regret in my life it is the worry I have given to my mum.

"I have to go mum, I`ll call or get word to you somehow, and let you know what is going on once I'm sure what's going on myself. Love you mum."

Through the runny nosed tears, she told me she loved me too and that was that. All I had was a two-minute phone call to tell my mum I was 'Banged up Abroad'.

If there was a time during my year in prison that I felt like crying, then it was at that moment. Not for myself but for my wee mum, for once again putting her through hell and adding more worry to the worry she already carried. She has had three men in her life. There was my father who died when I was ten, my brother who was murdered when he was only 34, and me, now sitting in a stinking Indian cell some 5,500 miles from home.

No boyfriends or other men in her life, she devoted it to her sons, and now one had been taken before her and the other, me, had gotten into a mess at the age of 44. It was all bound to have an effect on her.

That Monday I also had a rather surreal meeting with Advocate Raju. He had been sent by Peter D`Souza who would be defending me in my trial. He came along to the dungeon, and through the bars of the gates of the cell he asked me what had happened. I asked him what they said had happened, and lo and behold they had claimed I had been proceeding toward a drop off point to meet a customer with the bag with 2.75 kilograms of Charas.

I told him that wasn't true, but it didn't feel right speaking to him when standing right at his back was Punaji Gawas, the arresting officer and I.O in my case. It just wasn't right at all, and it would be some time before I got a handle on the Indian legal system and how it functions, or dysfunctions as it was going to turn out in my case. It took me some time to realise that the police and lawyers etc. are all different cheeks of the same big shitey arse.

Back in the dungeon and Johnny Cash, Scheme, and Pink Floyd songs about prison and time would not leave my mind. I had been listening to Cash and Scheme before my arrest and they were fresh, very fresh. "Time goes by, tick ticking away tick ticking away. Each minute seems a lifetime, this is my first today" ran round and round my mind. The only interludes were the sound of Johnny Cash telling San Quentin he hated every inch of it, and of Folsom Fucking Prison Blues. Because Johnny had shot a man in Reno, just to watch him die remember. The mind of James Toner has been a strange place over the years, but during that week in Panjim police lock up it went into overdrive. They say the mind produces between 50 and 70,000 thoughts daily, but the secret is to let them flow and not hold on to any of them, my thoughts that week were weird and wonderful and went from the sublime to the ridiculous.

People came and people went during the week, and I stayed there for a full 7 days. Gawas had told me he had the power to hold me there for 90 days, which I didn't fancy one little bit at all. Most days they took me along to their office, just to pass the time for them and me too, I suppose. We would go into Panjim to the medical centre every 2 days to make sure I was still ok for their custody, and when we were out they would buy me a wee samosa or something else that was a bit more advanced in the culinary stakes than the shite that came in the morning and again in the evening time.

It was all a big game to them, and if I`m honest, it was just a big game to me too. I had been in the game for around twenty years and it was my turn to be het. They had the wee mouse trapped, and I was that mouse. They took me out to play when it suited them which was most days. I just played along, because I knew not to let them know it was reaping havoc with my mind.

One day, one of the constables came along to my cell and told me it was time to go and have my photographs taken. I was to get my mug shots taken for official purposes. Again they took me along to the office and sat me down where I was given a black board to write my name and number on before having my snap clicked. I couldn`t see any camera, and what followed you couldn't make up. They told me we were going to the photo shop. I`m still thinking that's where I'm going to get them taken. I was right anyway, but didn't expect to be taken in to the city and taken to the Photo Click shop for the job to be done and my picture taken for police records. We had the pictures taken and then sat in the shop waiting on them being developed, me looking like I had been fired out of a gun and thinking all these bastards know I'm a prisoner, and that isn't right. Picture the grey looking white guy with the weeklong facial growth sitting with his name on his chalk board surrounded by Indian policemen. And I was worried what people might be thinking.

I most likely didn't make a scene cos I knew I'd be taken for a wee bite to eat and a fresh lime soda on the way back to the police station. The thing a man does to get a wee bit of fresh grub and a soft drink when in my position eh! I wouldn't have been sucking on any dick for the joy of getting something decent to eat, but I didn't mind looking like a lost soul being taken for a stroll on occasion. I was sure of that anyway. That ship called dignity had long since sailed in any case, the lack of facilities in Panjim had made sure of that.

Then back to the rat infested shite hole I called home for 7 days. At least I was being taken out for these wee walks, no one else was. They had to sit in that dark, stinking infested room for the whole time they were there. And they couldn't answer anyone back; I said what I wanted to who I wanted to by this point.

The fear had left me and I had accepted that this was to be my lot for the next week, then fuck knows what was going to follow after that. Gawas told me not to worry, but I would be in jail for a year or 15 months then I`d win my case. He told me he would make a weak case against me because I hadn't caused them any problems. It took me some time to understand why the arresting officer in my case would be telling me that I would be found not guilty because he would make the case against me weak.

Did I at that moment roll over and allow him to tickle my belly? I`m not sure, I can`t remember. Wee baw rub? Nah.

Various characters came and went, but one lad in particular was a good laugh. His name was Peter and he made it his vocation while there to kill as many mosquitoes as he could during the day so there were not as many out at night, actually makes sense. He roamed the cell throughout the day just skelping the walls with a rolled up newspaper. He succeeded in keeping the little fucking mossies down at night too. His English was good so we managed to converse quite a bit with one another, and that kept me going too during that first week.

He also told me what to expect of the place I was going next, Mapusa Judicial Lockup. He told me I'd be there a year before my case was over. He was right about the time in custody, but twenty-seven months after my release and at the time of writing this part of my story, I'm still in a legal limbo and no nearer the end of my case at all.

One of the funniest moments in the cell was when I woke for a dream that was induced by my withdrawal from the Charas. I woke from a crazy sleep and sweating like a madman, anyone who has ever stopped smoking hash will know what I mean by the sweats and bad dreams.

I had dreamt that we had managed to get a gun from some place and I had shot the guard dead. We were all set to escape, but I decided I needed a shite before I made a dash for it in my flip flops. In I went to the swamp for my last 'number two' in that hole, I thought. Maybe spread a wee bit of it over the walls for the next cunt to come along and wonder where it came from and what sort of clatty bastard would be doing that sort of thing. Anyway, I came out of the toilet to find the wee farmer fucking this dead police guard; he looked at me and in his broken English said to me:

"Sorry James, had to do this. But very sore because he has a tight tight Ghand and it is causing me some pain."

At that, I woke in a sweat thinking it was all real but very glad that we hadn't shot any policemen, I hadn't spread any shite over the toilet like the cunts before me had done, and I suppose even more relieved that wee Raj and everyone in the cell was fast asleep, and that the policeman and my own backsides were still our own and not now the property of that little Indian farmer. Happy days really for all concerned, as far as my dream was concerned at any rate.

So that was my days in the first week in the dungeon at Panjim police station. Not nice, and with more than a touch of the unknown, and I didn't know if this was the good or the bad side of the Indian penal system. I was soon to find out when I got my move to Mapusa Judicial Lockup.

Now, before we move on, I feel I should explain something. Some of you may be a little confused reading this chapter. I mean, there I am scoring 3 kilos of shitty hash (and 400g of the good stuff) but once I've been arrested, you have me shouting my innocence on the 3kg (or the 2.75kg it turned out to be). If this had been me getting a pull on a trip fae London tae Glesga, then my hands would have been up and I would have taken what came my way. But what pissed me off, and pisses me off to this day, is how corrupt these cunts were, how they'd been working with that wee wank, Mahalaxsmi, how they changed the point of arrest, and how the whole shebang was sweet fuck all to do with justice, but just another way of extorting cash out of tourists or expats. So was I gonna make their life easy? Wis ah fuck!

Chapter 10: Mapusa Beach

I reckon I was more than little bit afraid when I faced the Judge the morning of Saturday 30th May 2009. She didn't say much when she remanded me to judicial custody for 14 days. I was under no illusions about me having any sort of chance at all of receiving bail, my lawyer had told me to get that out of my mind totally, and that's what I did. I had no chance of getting bail and had best just accept my situation for what it was. I was fucked I suppose, totally fucked.

I still maintained I had been at no bus stop in Chapora, I still do. I still found myself heading to Mapusa judicial lock up and this shit hole was to be my home for the next 5 months. Little did I know that first day at Mapusa that I would actually ask to be transferred back to this little jail, a small holding unit that afforded no room for exercise or any real movement whatsoever.

That Saturday in May, I reached Mapusa about half past one in the afternoon and was taken to the reception area, a wee office that served a multitude of different purposes as it was to turn out. I can`t remember the officer who processed me that afternoon, but I do remember the guard who was on duty and the look on his face when I dropped my trousers and boxers for him to have a 'right good look'.

"Pull your pants up." He demanded.

"I thought you wanted a look the way you were touching me," was my reply, at the same time as spreading the cheeks of my backside as far apart as I could.

"Stop it James Toner." He snarled.

Turned out his name was Babu, and in the end he was a proper good guy in a right shite underpaid job. He in fact brought a bit of the Charlie Chaplin to Mapusa with his comic antics.

"Stop touching me, and then I will pull my trousers up." I told him and looked at his boss at the same time.

I was letting them both know that the only power they had over me was the power to lock me up and take away my freedom. They would not and could not take my dignity away from me. I was the only one who could allow that to happen and I had no intention of doing so.

They asked all the relevant questions and the officer told me what would be expected of me in his jail. I told him he would get no problems from me, and as long as I was treated properly it would remain that way.

I was allocated room number 2 in Mapusa J.C, and as I trudged along the corridor to my new abode it was not without some trepidation if I'm completely honest. I knew not what to expect when I got there.

Room number 2 was a big room by jail standards, well the standards I had experienced in my short time in jail in

Scotland when I was younger, but that did not really prepare me for the conditions I was about to face.

The guard opened the gate and put me in the room where I was met by 18/19 starring faces, all of Indian origin. Not one foreigner in sight was my first thought when I entered.

Standing with my 'bed block' in the middle of the room, I felt like the "spare prick". I didn't know what to do, and looked around the room for some sort of guidance. That came from one local Goan gentleman by the name of DD, and a total gentleman he was for sure.

I put out my hand and told him my name was James.

"We know who you are James, we have been waiting on you arriving now for a week." He said with a nice smile.

He went on to say that he knew, as did everyone else, all about my case and that I didn`t have to discuss it with anyone else who might be nosey enough to ask about it.

At the time I thought that it was awfully nice of this man to take the time out to sort of welcome me to Mapusa, but as time went on in there for me I began to realise what it was all about. I was to witness many 'interviews' in my time in the Indian penal system, but I'll get to them at some point in the tale anyhow.

DD pointed to a wee corner in the room and told me that unfortunately because the room was over crowded, the very corner of the room was where my floor space was to be. He told me that as people left I would be moved round to a 'more comfortable' spot on the floor, irony without any hint of subtlety at all those words were.

I put my bed stuff down on the floor and was shown the shower room. The shower room was a small corner of the main room which had been blocked off by some bricks to afford a certain degree of privacy to those of us who had to use this small space to wash, use the toilet, and do the dishes too. Not so clean that concept at all. The toilet was Indian, hole in the ground. The shower was a bucket of water with the water being splashed over you by use of a plastic jug.

I showered and dried myself before once again stepping into the main part of the room to be met by lots of staring Indian eyes.

I rolled my bed out in my corner and fell fast asleep, it was the first bit of real sleep I`d had since my arrest a week earlier. I was woken by someone shaking my leg and telling me it was exercise time if I wanted to come out into the yard. I knew I had to go to the yard at some point and I thought it best to get it over and done with as soon as I could.

I could not have been more wrong in what I imagined I was going to find out there as I entered the yard from the dark corridor into the blinding pre-monsoon sunshine.

"Dobra Udra." I heard as I walked slowly into the fresh air. I looked up to see this figure standing in his boxer shorts and pouring a jug of water over his head.

"Welcome to Mapusa Beach." He said to me.

"Nice," was all I could manage back at that point.

I had to stifle a smile all the same when I looked at this man properly. Standing in his knickers and soaking himself at 'Mapusa Beach'. He was about 6 feet tall and had shoulder length blonde hair. I couldn't help think he had all the look of a 'man cub' as he stood in front of me. And that's how I still know Viktor the Russian; he will always be Mowgli to me.

The short time in the yard went past in a hazy blur. There were people coming up to me and saying hello, some asking if I remembered them, and some telling me they knew my friends. All of this is typical jail bullshit which was made all the worse by the fact I was in India and in jail in a foreign country some 6000 miles away from my family and friends. The one thing I was sure of even at that early stage, was that this experience would not last forever, that it had no permanence. Just like everything else in this life we live.

That day passed in a bit of a blur, but I do know that I met some proper snakes in those short muddled up moments in the exercise yard. The first was Desmond D` Souza, a 55-year-old Goan smack head. No other term to describe him at that moment, so I make no apologies for using that expression. He slithered up to me in the yard that first day and delivered a classic sucker punch.

“Hello James. Don’t you remember me?”

“Not really, although your face is a bit familiar.” Of course it was familiar, because it’s one of those faces you see in any town or city in the UK, one ravaged by years of heroin abuse.

“I know you from before.” He hissed. “I know you and your brother, Martin”.

This cunt knew his stuff for sure.

“Where do you know me and Martin from?” I asked back. Not without getting a wee feeling that I didn’t like from this snake even at that first hazy introduction.

His reply did surprise me, because it could only have come from someone who knew me and my brother well enough during our time in Goa together back in the day before the locals became too greedy and began spoiling the place for everyone else. You might be thinking it was the tourists who spoiled places like Goa, and you would be in part correct, but the greed of the locals has more than contributed to its partial demise.

“I know you both from Nelsons Bar in Anjuna.” Answered ‘The Snake’.

He could only have done so if he had met me and Martin in Anjuna years ago, and we did both frequent the bar he mentioned.

He was also aware of the fact that Martin was dead and he didn't hear that from me for sure.

We were in the same room so we could continue our talk inside I told him.

I continued to circle the small yard and was introduced to a multitude of different folk during that time. One of them was another man who just had this creepy jail informant look about him. I know you might be thinking what does a jail informant look like, but anyone who has ever been in prison will know; a permanent look of fear, fear that they are about to be found out.

He went by the name of David Abraham, an Iranian National who had Indian Citizenship. The Snake warned me to tell him nothing and to be very careful of him. He was not a nice man apparently, rich indeed coming from this bastard.

The Arab, as he was called in Mapusa, told me he knew me too.

It was obvious he didn't, but I ran with it at first till I got my bearings in the place. I wasn't sure about him from the start but would find out for myself in the forthcoming months that he was not my cup of tea. The Arab knew some of my friends, he told me, but on reflection he was just mentioning Scottish folk he knew in the hope I knew them as well. In the days and months, I spent with him I would discover he was just another prison chancer.

An hour in the sun and then it was back to the gloom that was Number 2 in Mapusa. I felt a bit more relaxed this time, and all the staring faces were now smiling in the knowledge that "The Puklha" didn't bite. Well little did they know that he did, and with all the tenacity of a young Rottweiler. Fortunately, the teeth only had to be bared and any tension soon left the room in a flash.

That first day in Mapusa I also met Alesandro Castro or Milana as I knew him. He was a 55-year-old Italian, and although we had our moments as well during the 11 months I spent with him, I will not forget the gesture he made that first day at Mapusa Beach. After the exercise period, he came along from his own cell and produced this little bag of goodies for me. Some biscuits, powdered diluting orange juice, and a few wee other luxuries that he would have known I hadn't had in my week in the Panjim dungeon. I really thought that was a nice thing of him to do, and apart from the one time we came to blows, I more than repaid him for his show of empathy and generosity.

Back in number 2, the other lads were playing cards or a board game called Karam. I declined the offer to play and lay down again to try making sense of my surroundings.

The room was big I suppose, but not so big that we had any sort of space to call our own. I`d say about 8 yards square with the back corner built in to incorporate the toilet area. The toilet space was 1 yard by 2 yards, and did afford some degree of privacy when showering or using the actual hole in the ground. The door went three quarters of the way up the height of the wall, but not all the way to the top. There was a tap on the wall that was used to fill a large bucket, from which the prisoners were allowed 2 buckets each to use to wash once a day.

All around the room were little handmade boxes filled with people's possessions, and pictures of various Gods on the walls of the cell. Hindu and Christian all stuck to the wall with homemade glue. The glue was made by mixing bread and water and it eventually turned to paste, don't eat white bread.

Everyone in the room took time to stare at the foreigner who had come into their midst, and was not making too many friendly gestures at that point.

Around the back of 5, the shout went up that it was food time, and I fully expected the worst. I was not to be disappointed.

The food at Mapusa was brought in to the jail by an outside caterer who had the look of a man who didn't really want to be doing the job he was, but who had stumbled onto a good thing in terms of financial gain. His name was Mungledas, and more than once in my time at Mapusa I had to tell him to get his ladle to the bottom of the pot or he`d be wearing it. Saying this in an aggressive Glasgow accent with a few well-placed expletives always had the desired effect on this poor excuse for someone who could prepare and cook food for up to 70 prisoners at a time.

We all had a metal plate and a metal cup, and on the command, not really a command, we all trooped out in to the yard to get our "Khana", the Hindi word for food. That consisted of a cup of watery Dahl, a vegetable dish, and a couple of chapattis. The non-veg option was a couple of small not very fishy looking fish. At that point I was pure veg and continued to be so long after my release from jail, it seemed like the cleaner and safer option in terms of my health at the time.

Back in number 2, I was pretty hungry and sat down to eat my dinner right away. This was not the way of things in Indian jails though as I soon found out. All the other lads covered their own food with old newspapers and looked at me as if to say "not now Jim". I followed suit, and one of the lads told me we had a bath first before we all sat and ate together So not only did we eat this shite food, but we left it till it had no heat left in the dish as well, fucking great I thought.

The next couple of hours passed and my turn for the bath soon came around. I loved the way they called it a bath, it still brings a smile to my face even to this day. A bath it was not, far from it. 2 buckets of cold water and a bar of poor Indian government soap does not a bath make.

About 8 at night, when all the praying and bathing was over and done with, and the Catholics and Hindus had prayed to their Gods to be rescued and saved from the hell they found themselves living in, we all sat down in a big circle and began to eat our dinner.

I was the focal point of the meal, and the fact I wasn't the best with the fingers made sure all the rest of the prisoners had a laugh at my attempt. I was ok with that, and they weren't slow in showing me how they did it, to be honest I could be eating with my fingers for the rest of my life and it would not look or feel as comfortable as the Indians make it look. Messy as fuck as well.

It was at this time I began to realise that this eating with one hand and wiping (your arse) with the other was the way it was to be for me. Toilet paper was not allowed in Indian jails, the jail manual said so. I now believe that my backside has never been so clean in all my life and I will never use paper to wipe in my life again. If you are running through the meadow, (you should be attempting to imagine this) and you fall and land on a big bit of cow dung, you don't go home and wipe your hand with paper do you? No you don't, you wash it thoroughly with soap and water, sorry to digress. I was explaining the eating process at Mapusa Beach.

After dinner there was a small queue to get into the toilet to clean the plates and put them away till Mungledas came back in the morning with our breakfast. I was standing in the queue when one of the younger Indians grabbed my plate and proceeded to wash it for me, I was so embarrassed.

“No thanks.” I told him.

“No problem Uncle.” He replied. Remember, Uncle is used as a term of respect afforded to people older than you in India. I looked around, and no one seemed to be taking much notice of the younger lad and me speaking about him doing my dishes for me.

I know that in prison, as in pretty much every other walk of life, you don’t get anything for nothing so I was expecting the rub at some point off this boy. Turned out he didn’t want anything more than some butter and biscuits from the weekly canteen that we all had access too. You could only use the canteen if you had money to buy from it of course. The first week I had money, but after that I had a small problem waiting on my friends, real friends, coming over from Scotland and bringing with them money for me to get by during my time in prison in India.

The first weekend in Mapusa really dragged in; no amount of shit Indian TV could have made it worse.

Desmond attempted to cement his relationship with me by offering me tobacco, but I don’t smoke it. He hung about my wee small area for most of that first weekend like a bad smell, in fact that just about sums Desmond up. A bad smell.

He began to slip the odd wee bit in to the conversation about my case and how he could perhaps help me out. He didn't want to confide in me totally because he wasn't sure if he could trust me. Fucking classic reverse psychology that was, and the thing is at that moment in my prison experience he had me... almost. Unfortunately for him I had seen all sorts of cases like The Snake in my time in the shitty drug business in Scotland.

That is not to say that I totally dismissed him when his rub eventually did come.

"James Baba, I have a friend who could help you in your case."

"Why hasn't he helped you in yours then?"

"I don't have the money to pay him James." Desmond hissed.

"He must be a right good friend then?" I said to him in my best sarcastic Glaswegian tongue.

"What do you mean?"

"I mean if he`s your friend and he can't help you if you don't have money, then he's not really your friend, is he Desmond?"

"He has to pay the judge." He replied.

I was up for this at this point I should tell you all. I wanted to hear that someone in here could help me to get out of this mess I found myself in. I wanted to hear that the judge was bent and could be got at. The thing that held me back at that point was the fact that Desmond didn't have an arse in his own trousers. He had neither a pot to piss in nor a window to throw it out of. Still, he almost had this wideo falling for his shite.

He even at one point brought the details of his wife`s bank account in which the money was to be deposited. The thing that gnawed away at me was his insistence that I tell no one of the plan. I was especially not to mention it to David the Arab. Desmond told me David was not to be trusted, and David told me the same about Desmond. At that point I in fact trusted no cunt any fucking way, and I had made my mind up that Desmond was at it and would be getting nothing from me.

As the days passed in Mapusa, I settled down pretty quickly and tried my best to keep my head down and try not to think about anything that might or might not be happening in the outside world. I had no wife or girlfriend, so I did not have that age old problem of worrying about what, where, and with whom that men in prison torture themselves about. Thank the heavens for that.

I had my wee ma and my son Martin to think about, but I soon learned that if I thought about loved ones and friends it only increased the tension levels we all felt in jail. I was able to let it go with both hands and get on with the task in hand, surviving in a jail miles and miles away from them, and on this occasion out of sight out of mind is appropriate.

I was told not to count days, and that the days soon turned to weeks and the weeks to months. And that's the way it was for me. Every day in the jail is pretty much the same, any jail. Some fucker opens your cell up and some other fucker locks it. They are only doing their job, but it's hard to get that into your head when they are locking you up, and you are the one who is being told when to go to sleep and when to wake back up in the morning.

Desmond, the bloke I mentioned before who was attempting the hit on me for the money to get out of the jail, was by now really getting on my nerve ends. He even had the guts, balls, cheek, or audacity to tell me he had been dreaming about my brother, Martin. He never did find out how close he was to getting it at that point.

At every given opportunity, he would slither over and ask if my friend was ready to put the cash in his account yet, because the judge wouldn't wait forever. I told him I was waiting on money arriving from Scotland, and when I got it I would make up my mind what to do with it. The options were to keep it to pay part of my lawyer's fees or give it to this little squirming rat-faced looking Goan heroin addict. It isn't really much of a dilemma when you think about it.

I began to despise this little skinny fuck with all my heart, and it was only the arrival of a Greek bloke that saved Desmond from being stabbed in the eye with my pen. The Greek's name was Antony, and he arrived in some state; he had been in Goa for almost 30 years and could not believe that someone had fired him into the police. He was distraught and a definite suicide risk. I watched him 24 hours a day and no way was I going to let him top himself, not any hope in hell of that happening, not on my shift anyway. He was the Greek stereotype, dark and not an ugly bloke, but so full of himself. He asked me one day who I thought he looked like. I wasn't sure and told him so.

"Some people say I look like Amir Khan" (a famous Bollywood actor). I told him I knew the Khans but wasn't sure which one was Amir.

"My English friends say I look like Rowan Atkinson." Picturing Mr. Bean I had to admit that he did indeed look a bit like him. In the weeks to come he probably wished he hadn't said that to me because when I looked at him I didn't see Blackadder, I saw Mr. Bean.

He had a girlfriend outside, and all he did was worry about what she was up to, as it happens she was being fucked by some Italian 'friend' of theirs, but that wasn`t apparent at that point. Tony was all wrapped up in her, and all he went on about was this Greek model that he was going to give a baby to and marry when he got out of jail. I told him to forget her for the time being because she was no good for his head. He went on about her all day every day, and that is not a good place to be in jail.

So when he had settled down a bit, he spoke to me about Desmond. I told him I was going to take his eye out when he was asleep, call that what you like, but I was going to stab a human being in the eye with a dirty pen while he gouched away. Antony, who still spent a lot of time looking at the bars on the ceiling, put it all into perspective for me one day and saved Desmond from being blinded or perhaps even worse.

"James brother, he is fucked. He has no one outside and no one in here either." That was his slant on it.

"So fuck, he tried to rob me for 3 fucking laks." I reminded him. One lak is 100,000 rupees. At that time 3 laks would have been about four thousand British Pounds.

"Yes he did, but it wasn`t a personal thing with you and him, he would have tried the same with me but I know him from before. You shouldn`t take it personally because he is out to fuck anyone and didn't pick on you personally".

"He mentioned my brother's name and said he`d had a dream about him." I reminded Antony. "That was wrong, and it's that which is going to mean I stab the skinny fuck in the eye, you or no one else in here will stop me from doing that to him, Tony."

"Let's speak to him." Said the Greek"

“Get him over then.” I said.

Try imagining this in a Greek accent if you can.

“Desmond, are you fucking stupid?”

“What do you mean?”

“How can you get anyone out of here, you are a fucked up junkie with no one”.

“I`m going to kill you, Desmond, take your eye out with this pen when you’re lying full of your tablets or your smack, you try to fucking rob my lawyer’s money you cunt”.

Tony stepped in at this point and told Desmond to go to his bit of the floor and not to come near me for a while.

I was still going to take the eye out of the sleekit bastard at the first opportunity and he knew it, so it wasn’t long before he came over and attempted to make his apologies.

“James, I thought I could help you out, God’s promise.”

“You mentioned my fucking brother in a dream, ya prick, that’s what going to get you the kicking of your life, and I don’t see you getting much help from your fellow countrymen.”

By this point in my life I was sort of on my spiritual path, and I couldn’t help feel sorry for the skinny wee guy who had tried to fuck me for all my lawyers’ money. He sat in front of me and cried.

"I am so sorry but my friend let me down."

"Listen Desmond, you're either sorry or you're not, fuck your friend, and if you stay out of my way I'll stay out of yours."

"By the way Desmond, the Greek saved your eye from being poked out, you owe him one."

"What do you mean by that?"

"I was for taking your eye out with a pen, but the Greek convinced me that you are just out to fuck anyone and I should not take it to heart."

He just couldn't look at me, I think he was genuinely relieved to still have 2 eyes, can't blame him for that and I also felt a touch of embarrassment from him. He was a sick addict remember, and he had been caught so I can understand his slight feeling of shame.

Life in Mapusa was like Groundhog day, same shit different day to be honest. Woke at half 7 or before, tea and 2 dry rolls, then an hour walking in a circle which they called our exercise time. Depending on how many bothered their selves in getting out of bed, there could sometimes be 30/40 people walking round in the wee circle, hands in pockets and chatting away. All shaking hands and wishing each other a pleasant day, I know, but they were genuine in their good wishes to one another.

They had learned acceptance and impermanence. I was still to fully grasp either concept, and to be honest even sometimes now 3 years later, I still think my experience will never come to an end. I know it will, but it's easy enough to say but not so easy to actually accept.

In Mapusa I met one of the dirtiest evil men I had met in a life of meeting dirty evil bastards. His name was Ashpak Bengre, and he ran Mapusa JC. He was a murderer and extortionist. contract killer, gang leader, and all round general cunt. He was on remand for murder, his second term in jail on remand for another murder from which he walked free. Please, google this bastard.

He was another one who had introduced himself in the yard to me.

"Hello James, we have been waiting on you coming to Mapusa."

I didn't really think much about his words, but with the benefit of hindsight I was being told by the jail boss he knew who I was, and that in his head I was going to be one of his victims. Their favourite tricks with foreigners is 'can you buy me this or that from your canteen, my money hasn't come yet', or general shite like that. Most foreigners in an Indian jail would buy the deodorant or the biscuits or whatever the cunts were after. I chose to tell them no and see how it went from there.

Tony the Greek was a nervous wreck for most of the time we spent together, and would have been bad back up had it kicked off at all in Mapusa. Frail and rattling for whatever his medicine had been outside, and wouldn't have been any good in a fight.

David the Arab was one of those sorts that would have told you he`d be in like a flash, but in reality he would have cowered into a ball and pretended to sleep. He didn't like Bengre, but did a fair bit of licking his backside none the less. The Arab was also the jail medicine man, which meant he went round and distributed the medicine to the inmates who were due it. He was also a fly man and a thief, so if you were in with him he`d give you some other poor guys medicine and tell him all his was gone, and he`d have to go to the hospital the next day. So the Arab would make sure I had a wee sleeping tablet or a bit of hash or anything of that ilk, which he had procured from some other poor dude who needed them and had been prescribed them from the jail doctor who came round once a week.

Foreigners only had to shake the gate, say we didn't feel good, and we were whisked off under escort to the nearest hospital to tell of chest infections and total insomnia. Away we went with our codeine and our sleeping tablets that they gave foreign prisoners like sweets and juice to sedate us. Better to have me sleeping than winding up the guards and everyone else for that matter.

"Why are you always smiling James Toner?" The guards would ask.

"Does it annoy you that I smile?"

The prisoners would laugh and wait for the reaction, because one word from them and they would have been beaten by a big bamboo cane.

I`d wait until they put their canes down and run away with them, holding them through the gates of the dangerous prisoners and being begged by the guards not to give them the canes. The Indian name for the bamboo cane is Lahti, and the police are fond of giving out bamboo massages which are as they sound. Being massaged (beaten) by some fucking dwarf of a bully with a thick bushy moustache is not my idea of fun. Having said that, I can say this right here and now though, never once was I mistreated by any of the policeman who framed me or by any of the guards who looked after me. I gave them no real reason, and it wasn't a great idea for them to go hitting foreigners anyway. I just kept them on their toes and to make sure they knew I was not afraid of them, any of the prisoners, or anything they could do to me. They couldn`t touch a foreigner because it would have brought to much trouble onto them, so they didn't touch any of us, except some Nigerians who did get stroppy at times and who ended up in the psychiatric hospital and came back like zombies. I don't know what they were being fed but it didn`t look like it would have been allowed in a British prison, the Largactyl shuffle springs to mind.

As I was to find out later in my time in jail, they gave you anything to sedate you, and sometimes sedation is better than being locked up 22 hours a day with some total arseholes. I was fucking sick of hearing my name being said out loud, James Toner office, James Toner visit, James Toner hospital.

My name is fucking James, simple as that, I would say. Almost drove me mad that as well.

Anyway, my time at Mapusa continued, and me and Antony the Greek were becoming even more annoyed at being in the big cell that was room number two. It was a transit cell and people were coming and going all the time. That has some psychological effect in itself, people being let out of jail while you know nothing of your own fate. People waiting on and getting their bail, shaking hands with guys while inside your own wee head you were attempting to turn things around with thoughts like: that wee bastard getting bail and you are still stuck here. It was slowly but surely getting to me, it had already got to Antony. He used to like his sleeping pills so was never in a very good mood in the morning anyway, but when that television went on at seven in the morning and the full place was up having their breakfast, he snapped. I was woken one particular morning by his screaming at the top of his voice. There was Mr. Bean shouting away in Greek, the only word of which I know is

Malakas. It's Greek for wanker. If he didn't look so ludicrous, I`m sure he would have been beaten by the other Indian prisoners. They are very cliquish and would have beat Antony up for his noise and obvious bad words. He also liked to use the word Mongoloid to describe all the Indians in the jail, but especially one in particular, Jayesh Dhuri. Mongoloid is not a word I would use, but this Jayesh was and most likely still is one total clown. Me and him crossed swords later on during my time there, but I put him in his place and he shat it, Antony was right he was.

One day The Greek came to me and told me that he had organised a move from the big room into a smaller room. The only problem was that it was Ashpak Bengre`s room, and moving in there was literally like getting into bed with the devil. I weighed up the pros and the cons and decided to go for it. The only problem I had was that his room was only big enough for eight men and it was already full. Antony told me that was no problem because Ashpak was going to throw two guys out of the room, no doubt in his mind to make way for the rich pickings from foreign lands.

I decided that I would take the chance and go to the room that was known as Ashpak`s room. Well it must have been, because he had just gone down to the head jailer and told him that Antony and I were going to be replacing two other men who I at first found it difficult to look in the eye. Ashpak and Antony had reasoned that they were either soon to be freed or convicted and would be moving from Mapusa in any case. I told myself that was the case, but I did feel a bit of guilt and a touch embarrassed as well as it happens.

I felt that not only was I getting into bed with the devil, I was also kicking two guys out of it for the pleasure of doing so, it didn't sit right with me until I spoke to one of them.

His name was Sam, an Indian from another state. That made him below me in the jail order as it turned out as well. I was a foreigner remember, Antony was as well. Sam was in for an alleged American Express cheque fraud attempt, everyone used to have a laugh with him about that. He didn't look or sound American but he had used a stolen and tampered with American passport to try and carry out his bit of fraud. He had pulled up outside some money exchange in an auto rickshaw and attempted to cash $2000 of stolen cheques.

The man in the shop saw through his 'cunning ploy' straight away and called the police. Sam was arrested in the shop ten minutes later. His case was almost over, and he had in fact attempted to enter a guilty plea, but the judge wouldn't allow him to, stating she would have no alternative but to sentence him to three years in jail if he pled guilty.

He was a well-educated bloke who spoke very softly, and I approached him in the yard soon after I took his place on the floor of the devil's room. I asked him how he felt about being moved on my account from a room that he had been in for months. He was almost emotional when he responded.

"I feel as if I was singled out and I have done nothing wrong James." Said Sam.

"I know that Sam, but you are moving soon and we thought you wouldn't mind because we are going to be here for another year at least".

"Please don't say to Ashpak that I am upset about being forced to move, James." The look in his eyes was one of a man who knew he could do nothing about being told to move, fear tempered with more than a touch of sadness.

I promised him I wouldn't say anything to Ashpak or anyone else and we shook hands on it and no more was said about it. Around three weeks later, the judge who refused to accept his guilty plea found him guilty and sentenced him to six months. He had already served more than that, so left Mapusa a free man.

As it turned out, Sam was a habitual fraudster who wasn't good at it and would be back in Mapusa before I had the chance to leave the place. I would meet Sam again in the months to come.

The first night in 'Ashpak`s room' was a strange one, we all got stoned but I didn't feel relaxed at all. He did everything he could to tell me to relax, and told me in a couple of days I would feel right at home. He was right about that too as it t turned out. The actual night itself was hilarious. The Greek had a good bit of Charas and we all got stoned, properly high in our new environment.

Viktor the Russian hadn't smoked for a long time so he was particularly stoned, and I made the mistake of pointing out the Mr. Bean like antics of Antony. Antony was furious about this, but Viktor did not stop laughing and kept pointing at The Greek who was posturing and telling Viktor to stop it. I should point out that Viktor was not the brightest star in the sky, and he laughed and shouted all night. Antony didn't help matters because when he told one of his many stories he made all the same facial expressions and gestures of Rowan Atkinson, who incidentally I think Antony meant rather than Mr. Bean. That was one of the funniest moments in my time in jail in Goa and one I will never forget.

Chapter 11: I Am Number 6.

I was now in room number six, and it had a rather cosmopolitan feel to it, I'm smiling as I write that.

We had Japanese, Russian, Italian, Greek, Nepali, an Iranian of Indian Citizenship, Indian, and me. There were eight of us in all in a much smaller but cleaner room. My space on the floor was between Alex the Italian and Viktor the Russian who had been playing at Mapusa beach on my first day in the Jail.

Better conditions for sure, but I was soon to find out that the dynamics of the room were set by a socio/psychopathic Muslim who kneeled and faced Mecca five times a day and made his Namas. I`m not against that at all but he was a five-time murderer who had been a member of the Infamous D Company of the Bombay Mafia who killed and extorted poor people for his own financial gain. I`m not sure what the Prophet Mohamed said when he came out that cave with the words Allah wanted him to pass on, but I would hazard a guess that there is nowhere in the Koran that allowed for such behaviour.

I asked him how he felt about that during one of the many conversations we had, and his answer was that he would be judged alongside everyone else when the day of reckoning came. No remorse, but as I said he was a psychopath, I have met many in my day who I would have called a psycho, but in Mapusa I got to live with one at close quarters and I took the time to study his behaviour in the short time we spent together.

I watched as he put the fear of God into Alex with his constant veiled threats about what was going to happen when he got his ten years. Alex had no money or very little, and Ashpak didn't allow him to forget it. He would ask who the Charas belonged to that Alex was smoking, he knew fine well but just liked to make the guy feel bad. Alex in turn would ask him to stop it and give him some peace, but most of the time he just took his psych hospital prescribed Amitriptyline and slept the time away, no doubt hoping that the constant berating by this nutcase would stop. And one day that's exactly what happened, it stopped, though when I say it stopped he merely transferred it onto Antony.

To be fair, Antony brought it all on himself by his constant getting into his business with Ashpak. He even gave him money to arrange his escape, but as you can imagine that never happened. He also gave Ashpak too much information about his girlfriend, and how he was worried about her and what he would do if she ran away while he was inside. Antony hung himself out to dry, and the cunning bastard that Ashpak was just turned up and picked what he wanted for himself.

I wasn't a party to the escape plan, I can only imagine Antony would have been told to tell no one about it or he would lose the money that his girlfriend had already paid in advance, the rest of which would have been paid once the job was done. The escape in itself would have not been difficult to pull off, but I believe that if he had been picked up and helped out, then he would have been killed once he had paid the money to Ashpak`s men outside.

This is how the plan would have worked, it was simplicity in itself and anyone of us could have run away if that was what we wanted to do. I never planned it, but I did think about it every time I was escorted to the international telephone once a week, but that's as far as I got. In any case, Britain would have sent me back the first time I set foot on her Britannic Majesty`s soil.

Two old policemen used to come to the jail to escort you to the international telephone which was round the back of the jail. They were always old guys whose police careers were almost at an end, or young guys who were just beginning in that sorry underpaid excuse for a job. They were not allowed to handcuff you, and in fact didn't pay much attention to the prisoner at all during the five-minute walk round the corner to the wee shop.

Antony had paid two Laks up front, and on more than one occasion he expected a couple of Ashpak's henchmen to be waiting to spring him when he was coming out of the shop. Threaten the guards, who wouldn't have been too interested in getting beaten, and drive off with Antony in a waiting car. They would then have taken him over the Goan border into one of the neighbouring states and collected the rest of their wages.

I could feel the tension increasing in the room between them, but Antony had told him where the girlfriend stayed, allowed her to meet with someone to give them the deposit, and in doing so had left the pair of them vulnerable to an evil murderer like Ashpak Bengre.

I would watch them both walking round the small yard deep in conversation, and could see the growing concern and embarrassment on Antony`s face. He had lost a fair bit of weight, and used to pull his trousers right up over his stomach to hold them up, Mr. Bean yet again. In the end I asked him what the problem was.

He told me about the plan, and that it hadn't happened the twice he was expecting it to. He had asked Ashpak for his money back, but Ashpak told him it was the guys outside who had fucked them both, and he couldn't get any money back from them. He played the fear card and told him that his girlfriend could be at risk from these guys if he made any noise about the situation.

I told him that he was fucked and to forget it, what was he going to do about it? He couldn't face up to Ashpak, he was afraid of him, and it showed in the way he spoke to him and the way he looked at him when Bengre spoke to him. It wasn't as if he could tell the police about it either, so the best thing he could do would be to forget it altogether and don't trust anyone in here again.

That was actually one of the very first things I said to Antony when he first came in one month after me. I told him to trust no one, not even me. If he decided he could trust me then fair enough, but at that very first moment even I could be the next one to fuck him over.

So as you can perhaps imagine things did get a bit strained in number six for a wee while. It got so bad for the Greek that he used to pretend he was asleep so that he didn't have to sit and face the smirking smile of that smarmy bastard. It was a smile that always carried a veiled threat when it spoke to Antony.

After a visit he would say to Antony, "How was Natasha today then Antony?"

"I like the way she wears her jeans, she has a lovely ass."

Antony would walk up and down the small space on the cell floor making himself demented, a constant look of worry on his face. Then he would lie down and pretend to be asleep in his wee space on the floor of the room.

One night Ashpak was going on about how he was going to get him moved to another room, and I told him if Antony went I would go with him. We had come together and would leave together. Antony was lying with his face to the wall but was not asleep, and Bengre said that he felt like giving him a beating.

I asked Ashpak to leave it out with him; I thought he had taken enough of a mental beating without having to endure a physical one as well. I thought it was time he got off Antony's back and that he should remember it was him that brought the two of us to the room in the first place. He never said another word to Antony after that night. Next day I told Antony I knew he had heard the conversation and he had better stay away from Bengre. Antony isn't daft and he kept out of Ashpak's way for the rest of our time in his room. They obviously had to pass the time of day with one another being in such close proximity, but the tension had been broken at least. I didn't yet realise it, but Antony was by this point broken as well.

The Arab, David, hated Bengre and the feeling was mutual. To be honest they both did very little to disguise it and just co-existed in peace because there was nothing else for it. The Arab, as it will transpire later in the story, turned out to be a proper dirty bastard, and as is the way of things with people like that, he got a sore one sometime later, not from Bengre and not in the form of physical violence. He got smacked in the back of the head with his own boomerang so to speak, threw it and forgot to duck when it came spinning back at him. I will get to that soon enough though.

The Russian, Viktor, was a space cadet as you may have already gathered by my first impression of him. He was a couple of years older than me, and when Perestroika came in 1989 and the walls came tumbling down, he took full advantage of it. Viktor set off travelling and found India, Goa to be exact. The charge was a big joke to him, and to the rest of us if the truth be told.

Viktor lived in the far North of Goa where many other Russians came and tried to settle, if only for the season for some. They loved their cocaine, or the adulterated version they would have been buying from the local or the Nigerian dealers in them parts. They would have been paying anything between 3500 and 5000 rupees for a gram of this stuff, and as their money was all black they hadn't been too badly affected by the 'credit crunch' of 2008, hence they were buying lots of this shite and having the time of their lives. No more queuing for a loaf of bread or a couple of slices of meat for this new generation of liberated capitalist Russians.

Viktor saw what he believed was a gap in the market, or at least the chance to get in on the game and make some money of his own into the bargain. He developed what he proudly called 'Magic Coke'.

He would simply buy the ingredients for his magic mixes from any of the pharmacies in the North of Goa where anything went. You could at that time buy almost any drug on the market over the counter in Goa. His mix was a simple one and very readily available.

He was buying Ephedrine pills and mixing it with some legal cousin of the cocaine family that was used to numb people's gums. He would crush the pills down and mix them with the legally bought benzocaine or whatever it was, and call it Viktor's Magic Coke. He sold his product for 2000 rupees a gram and the daft Russians who were kept up all night after two lines of it thought it was just that: Magic Coke.

In the end, it was another Russian dealer who had lost all his own customers to the 'Magic Coke' and who was working for the same ANC who arrested me that set Viktor up for his fall. He opened the door to the ANC one morning and they searched his house, in the fridge they found 250 grams of the legally bought powder and tested it the way that all cops on the TV in America test it. One dipped a finger in and rubbed it onto his gums, which then went numb because that's what the powder was intended to do, and Viktor was arrested and charged with being in possession of 250 grams of cocaine. He thought that story was hilarious, but didn't get that we were not laughing at the joke, he was the joke.

Viktor was oblivious to the goings on in the cell, I`m not sure to this day if he was genuinely thick and couldn't see the dynamics, or it was better for him to act as if he couldn't so he needn't get involved. Whatever the case, he smiled at everybody and had no real friends or enemies, the same as myself in a way, but me speaking English and being Antony`s friend had put me in the position where I couldn't watch him being bullied any longer.

The other two occupants of the cell were Yuki Morritta from Japan and Bim Lama from Nepal. Yuki was close to the Arab and that was to cost him dear in the months ahead, but he was a nice guy who would draw pictures of us and between them they kept the cell immaculate, well as immaculate as a cell in an overcrowded Indian jail can be. Yuki was always writing and always asking questions about English words, and if I knew the words of this song or that song, Nirvana mostly. At that point in my life I had never given Nirvana a second listen to and didn't realise the genius that Kurt Cobhain had been.

Yuki and I had bonded when we first met when I asked him if he knew Shunsuke Nakamura. His name is Nakamura Shunsukei, was the reply because apparently in Japan the family name is said first. You must be Celtic fan then, said Yuki. He was very deep though, and you could see that something was troubling him; I don't mean his impending court dates but something else. It would transpire that the Arab had shafted him for his lawyer's money and he was afraid that he would get ten years in an Indian jail. That would have been a result considering the place he was to end up after he was acquitted of the drug charge he faced in Goa. That's for later as well.

Bim Lama was this poor wee guy from Nepal; he had been caught with ten kilos of Charas but only charged with being in possession of one of them. The sentence for one kilo of hash is the same as it if for fifty kilos; ten years' rigorous imprisonment they called it. The police would have stolen the other nine kilos and used them to set up foreigners who had been caught buying smaller pieces, or given to the local Goan peddlers to sell for them. It was a win-win situation for the ANC; they got at least one arrest on their figures and made a few hundred thousand rupees to boot.

Bim had been in jail for around ten months before my arrest, and at the time of me writing this part of the story in July 2012 he is still in Vasco Sada Jail under trial. He has been in jail now for almost four years awaiting his fate. He will be sentenced to ten years because he has a government lawyer who won't really argue his case for him, and although he may be guilty of a crime, he should be set free because the police stole most of the Charas he was paid to carry. He knew what he was doing but he was never going to make it because he was another bit of cannon fodder. That's what I think about that in any case, I think about wee Bim now and then, and sometimes we bump into one another at court. He has been broken by this shite experience.

By now in Mapusa, it was early August 2009, and the monsoon was almost breaking, it rained now and again but not constantly as it did in July. The cell was about to get a bit of respite from the despot with the Moa/Hitler/ Stalin complex. Ashpak would be leaving the room for a wee while, at the time we thought it would be temporary, but in the end up it didn't work out that way. We were the fortunate ones.

About a week before the Muslim Holy time of Ramadan, Ashpak started speaking of moving in to a cell that would have only Muslims in it for the month in which people who follow that religion fast during daylight hours and eat only before and after the sun rises and sets. I thought he was kidding himself on, but he went and spoke to the jailer about it, and organised a bit of a reshaping of the various cells in Mapusa.

There were seven cells in Mapusa and he had 'commandeered' number seven for him and the rest of the people who wanted to fast and pray during Ramadan. Like I said, it suited all of us to a T and we were all glad to see the back of him. When he moved next door you could feel the tension that he had taken with him was gone from the room. It was like a non-violent revolution had taken place to remove a dictator, albeit in his own fucked up psychotic head. We got someone else and he left, simple as that.

To be honest, you could actually feel the tension in the whole jail had been lifted because Ashpak and the rest of the guys in room number seven never came out for exercise so we had no dealings with them. They were up early to eat and too tired or weak to come out during the day. It was bliss for the full 29 or 30 days it lasted that year. To be honest, Bengre coming back was always going to be a shite time, and the storm clouds gathered the day before Ramadan ended.

He approached me in the yard and told me he was bringing someone else to the room. He asked if I was ok with that.

“To be honest I’m not happy with that Ashpak, you know we are overcrowded as it is at the moment.”

“Don’t worry, we will fit him in and he will do all the cleaning and washing in the room” he reasoned.

“Fit him in where? There is no room on the floor for anyone else to come into the room, Ashpak, and if you do bring him then I will leave the room.”

He smiled and moved round the yard and spoke to the Arab, I don’t know what was said then but he seemed happier when he had spoken to him. I was going to move and that would be that. By this time, I was no longer the new foreigner in the jail, and I could speak to the staff and the jailer freely, so I would just make sure I went into one of the smaller rooms and not back into transit room number two. I had christened that room King’s Cross Station because of the noise and the amount of people who came and went almost on a daily basis.

The next morning came and I expected the scenario to be a bit different from the way it actually turned out. Ashpak came along to number six with this young Muslim lad who had been doing some serious press ups and dips by the look of him. I took one look at the two of them and stood up and began rolling up my bed and putting my gear into plastic bags that I had. The bemused guard didn't know what was happening but he was more afraid of Ashpak than he was of me and quite rightly so.

I told him to leave the gate open because I wasn't staying in a room meant for four or five maximum with nine people. As I walked towards the door with my bed I turned and could not believe my eyes. Everyone in the room except for the Russian was James Toner. I don't know who made Spartacus or I'd credit them for that line, but the show of solidarity was fantastic. If I moved, they were all going to move!

Bengre was furious and the look he shot me could have killed, remember he had at least five times before. I looked at the guard who was shitting himself, why was this happening on his watch he would have been asking himself. He locked the gate with us all in except for the young lad who was being brought to clean and wash Bengre`s clothes and plates and whatever doings he had in line for him.

The guard came back with the jailer who addressed me out of the crowd.

"James Toner, why are you making problems?" he grunted.

"Sir, with all due respect the room is too crowded with eight men, and if that boy comes it will be even more so. I will move to another room to save you the bother of any other problems."

He had a look at the other six men who would also want to move if I did, and then he spoke to Bengre in Konkani. None of us in the room spoke that language, so we had no idea what was being said about us. It didn't matter, because the young lad who was still standing there suddenly picked his own stuff up and walked back to the room he had come from.

I had won a battle, but at that point I thought I had perhaps started a war, I took no comfort when I looked at the face of the hired contract killer in front of me. He was fuming, livid, and struggling to contain his temper. That was the last time we spoke to one another, the rest of the day was a bit strained and the atmosphere could have been cut with a knife. Soon enough all of the jail would know about it, and that would only make the embarrassment factor even more of a danger to me.

At night time I had my usual wee puff from my home made pipe and took my sleeping pill and prepared for sleep. As I drifted off, I could hear the Italian and Bengre speaking, the same Italian who had rolled up his bed when I had rolled mine. I couldn't make out the words and drifted off into a nice wee warm medicinally induced sleep.

I was woken early the next morning by the sound of the gate being opened, and the sight of Bengre being helped by his wee chum to carry his bed and belongings along to the cell they had shared at Ramadan, Bengre was moving out of his 'own' room because of me. Things were going from bad to worse, and the situation that I thought had been bad enough the day before was now definitely turning into something that could quite easily have turned very nasty.

At eight o clock every morning, we were all allowed into a small yard about the size of a tennis court, Mapusa Beach was the name it was given on my first day there you might recall. I fully expected the confrontation to be straight away and put on my running shoes that tied in preparation for a fight that never materialised. Bengre didn't come out of his room that morning, nor again during the afternoon hour we were given to exercise as well. I knew it would come but wasn't sure when.

The mood in number six was very upbeat; we had totally overthrown the dictator and there were those amongst us who openly rejoiced. Antony was over the moon that his nemesis was not going to be there at every waking moment, the Arab too showed open signs of his own joy at the situation. I was a bit more subdued, because I knew it was me that was going to have to fight him in his own jail in front of his own fans.

Well the truth is Ashpak Bengre didn't have any fans, and if anyone did have a support it was actually me. I didn't set out to be Mr. Popular in Mapusa, but my nature and the fact I had accepted that I was going to be there for at least a year or more had made me many friends. The only trouble was that I didn't know what side they would be on if the fight kicked off, and if any of his wee cliques would become involved in it. I should remind you all that at that point all of this was just going on in my head and none of it had actually happened yet.

Again the next morning I went through the same getting up and putting my shoes on routine. By this time, I'm telling myself if he starts I`m going to get in close and get a grip of that long beard of his; he sported a big long Bin Laden style beard. If I could get a grip of that I wouldn't be letting it go until I had bitten his nose, ear, or any part of his face off being my thinking at that point. I suppose I was on the verge of being neurotic, but knew that the Indian who, in his eyes, I had betrayed and humiliated, would at some point want to even matters up with me.

Again that morning he stayed in his own cell, as a matter of fact he didn't come out of his cell for almost two weeks. I couldn't understand or believe it to be honest.

There was though a bit of tension created in the cell by the fact that the Italian was afraid of him, and when Bengre went down to collect his food, the Italian would stand at the cell door and shout hello to him. When we were opened up, he would go along and say hello to Bengre at his room number seven. It was starting to grate on my nerves, because I knew that Bengre was used to seeing this sort of thing, and I wasn't having the Italian allowing him to divide and conquer our little group.

It all came to a head the day Bengre did eventually decide to come out of his own wee cave. He made a point of walking past our group and saying hello to the Italian and the Russian. I looked him in the eye, and he made this big three-year-old child movement with his head to show he wasn't speaking to me. I thought to myself, what a fanny he actually is. The next thing, the Italian is up on his feet and walking round the yard with Bengre, who knew he had this cunt shitting himself and was using the age old Imperialistic British tactic of 'divide and conquer'.

That night when we were locked up for the night I had it out with him, but it went too far and ended in blows. I tried to explain what was happening to him but he wouldn't listen.

"Why are you speaking to Bengre?" I asked him.

"Why not, he said hello and we speak to each other." was his reply.

"Can`t you see that he is using you as a pawn in his game with the rest of us, why does he speak to you and not to anyone else? I`ll tell you why Alex, it's because he knows that you are afraid of him and he knows none of us are because we are all standing together."

"I can speak to whoever I want to speak with and it`s nobody's business."

I was beginning to fume at his attitude and told him so.

“Alex, you sit in here and smoke my Charas or his Charas and his cigarettes but you bring nothing to this party at all. We know you don’t have any money, but we still share what we have with you. You pay that back by walking round the yard with Bengre, so maybe you should move into his room then.”

He looked at me and spoke in his Italian accented English. “This is not your room so you cannot put me out of it.”

I agreed but told him he would be smoking no more Charas or cigarettes belonging to any of us in the room again.

He looked up at me and said “So fucking what.”

I snapped at that point, and jumped up in a flash and kicked him on the side of the head. He staggered back and I threw my weight on top of him, raining blows on him as he struggled to get me off him in his corner of the room. I felt myself being pulled back and eventually off him by the Russian who was big and very powerful.

I hadn’t done him any damage with my bare feet, and he was cowering to protect himself from my punches, but I was seething at his blasé attitude to something that was very serious. We were in an Indian jail and were in a very small minority. I almost laughed at his response to my attack when he called me a fuckin football hooligan.

I was frothing at the mouth and asking what his grandfather had done during the war and all sorts of shite like that, I had lost the plot momentarily and I had no control over any of my words or actions. The Russian had to hold me for ten minutes before I relaxed and promised I would stop it. That night I had to sleep on the floor in my usual place beside the Italian and the Russian, I slept but I'm not so sure that he would have had too much sleep that night.

I was fighting for my survival against someone who had murdered on more than five occasions, and I didn't think that I was in the wrong. I was a bit gutted that I had lost my temper and kicked a guy in the face, but now he knew how I felt about it and it was up to him if he wanted to take his chances in a rematch. To be honest, he was a wee wiry cut guy who would have given me a good fight but he had no heart for a prison yard scrap. I now understand that he was in the middle of the fight for his life and he was afraid of actual violence. Growing up in Castlemilk in Glasgow I had been surrounded by it, been a victim of it, and dished out some of my own.

I wasn't proud of and didn't like the feeling that it gave me when I could see that the Italian was as scared of me as he was of Bengre, not saying I was filled with shame, but it didn't fill me with pride either.

A couple of days later he wasn't going out for afternoon exercise, so I declined myself and left the pair of us in the locked cell together.

I took the opportunity to tell him I was sorry for resorting to violence, but that I still thought he was wrong in licking the arse of the devil that Bengre definitely was and no doubt still is.

Alex told me he had been thinking, and had a plan that he was going to fight me in the yard in front of everyone. I smiled and told him I was glad he didn't carry out that plan because in front of 40 or 50 men I would have been forced to fight as if my life depended on it, and I would have caused him damage that we would both have regretted. We shook hands and decided to speak no more about it, he could speak to whoever he wanted and he was also paddling his own canoe. If he spoke to Bengre about me I would not be happy, and I would have to put a pillow over his face when he was asleep and then everyone in the cell would have been in bother. We left it at that.

That was the only time I allowed my mind to run away with me in Mapusa. I was one of the fortunate ones; I had money for the canteen and to pay the guards to bring in my Charas too, I had a visit every week from Toff or Tommo, the latter a very ex-friend, from big Martin, another very ex-friend, and a couple from John Cass. The talk was mainly small, but I put that down to them thinking the worse for me and not wanting to say anything that would perhaps throw my mind into a dark place. All except Toff would have a wee shot at that later in the story as it goes. Toff was, and I`m in no doubt still is, a right good cunt.

The best visit during my time in Mapusa came not long after I was arrested, and it was one of my friends who had come over from Scotland to bring me some money to make sure I was ok while I was in the jail. At that time, we did not know how long that was going to be. I was expecting him, but when I walked in to small office that Tuesday morning I could have cried. I`d go as far as to say he did.

The shout went up for James Toner for a visit, and I walked along the small damp corridor looking forward to seeing wee Tosh. Me and Tosh had made a fleeting visit to India together one time before, so he sort of knew the way things were. He was obviously concerned about my welfare and state of mind, but I'm sure he left the jail that day under no doubt that both were just fine. I had lost a bit of weight cos the food was shite and dirty, but my mental health at that point was no worse than it had been when I left Scotland about two months previously.

I had broken the law and been caught, and I blamed no one but myself. He wanted to go to Vagator and kill Omkar Mahalaxsmi, the little fuck that had helped set me up. I no longer even consider him to be a little fuck.

One day I was at court, when my lawyer told me that a Scottish friend had called him and told him two of my friends wanted to visit me. I couldn't imagine who it was and thought a bit about that on the way back down to the jail. It was one of the fortnightly trips to the court that I had to go through for the six months before my charge sheet would eventually be served on me. I say go through, but anytime out of the jail is good time, and I was learning to manipulate the system to my own ends by this point as well.

As we drove up to the nearest point to the jail gate, I saw three figures standing with their backs to me, they turned round and one came walking towards me. Shook my hand and told me his name. I'm not giving his name here for a few reasons, but one day I hope to write that guy's story because it would put Shantaram to bed once and for all. No add-on or welded on legs and arms, just an honest account of one guy's extraordinary life.

He then scurried away and I turned to face the other two lads and couldn't believe it when I saw it was two young lads from Castlemilk. I wouldn't have called them friends or even associates, but they were two boys about twenty years younger than me who had a couple of weeks to spare and were going on holiday, so they decided to come and visit me in Goa because I was in the jail.

Dean and Paul, I thank you for that wee surprise visit, it brought a smile to my face and at the same time put the lacklustre efforts of people who were much closer to me at the time into perspective. They brought some Glasgow chat and a couple of books with them, although they didn't give me the Charas that they had been given to pass over to me, but they can be forgiven for that. Something very liberating in being able to speak your own language at your own speed without fear of anyone knowing a single word of what you are saying, and that is what we did on the two visits they paid me. Jabbered away in the harsh Glaswegian brogue that not one of the officers sitting could make out, to such a degree they asked if it was my own country's language.

I received lots of mail and sent the same amount back. In fact, I sent more than I received but that is probably the way it is when you are in the jail. I was to discover and make a mental note of the fact that I too had been guilty in the past of not keeping in touch with some of my friends who had been sent to prison. I promised myself that if the boot was ever on the other foot again I would be sure to take an hour at least once a week and write a small letter or take the ten minutes it takes to write a card. It is these little things that mean so much.

It was my mail, and the amount I received and wanted to send back out, that brought my first major confrontation with the jail management, the jailer. The procedure was that you gave your outgoing mail to one of the staff and he gave it to the jailer to censor. The jailer then got one of his men to post the letters; the post office box was right outside the jail. There was no need to go out the way for anyone and no extra staff required.

I had been in the office for one thing or another when I noticed my handwriting on three letters sitting on his desk. I asked why they were still there and had not been posted to their destination.

He flew into a fit of rage and started shouting and bawling at me, it was a wee shame really because he was an old man who didn't have long to go in terms of his prison officer days and he was attempting to show this foreigner he was the boss, one last attempt at convincing himself he had 'Power'. He beckoned me round to his side of the desk and produced the jail manual; up to this point I had only heard of the jail manual, and thought it was a figment of the imagination of the staff to put down any questions that they didn't or couldn't answer for themselves.

"The jail manual states that each prisoner has the right to one free letter per month which the government would pay for, and one that the prisoner could pay for himself, a total of two letters per month, James Toner. My men are not postmen, so go back to your room and I will have these posted when we have the time".

Now at that time I was writing perhaps three letters every week, so two per month did not sit too well with me. I returned to my cell and mused over the jailer's words and the fact that he had actually allowed me to see the jail manual at all. It was not the last time I would ask to see it during my time in Mapusa, or even after my transfer to Vasco Sada Jail at the end of October 2009.

Back in my room, I sat and thought about the events in the office, and looked around the cell; there was not one other person in that room who wrote a letter to anyone. That meant that there were seven free government letters not being allocated or used. I then had a look at the various other rooms round the yard. I knew of no one who actually wrote any letters at all, and was more than positive that none of them had ever had access to the jail manual that stated that they were all entitled to one free government letter per month. It wouldn't have made any difference to a lot of them because they were still signing for visits and anything official using their thumb print. Most of the out of state prisoners, and they were the majority, were illiterate in any case so they wouldn't need their free letter.

I sat down that night and wrote a letter to the jailer, they like to call it an application because it feeds their lust for power that their wee jobs give them. So it wasn't a letter I wrote to him, I made an application to him, and seeing how it was an application I mentioned the judge in it. The Narcotic Drugs and Psychotropic Substance (N.D.P.S.) judge has ultimate control over prisoners charged under that act. All that basically means is the judge has power over the jailer too.

I worded the application in a friendly manner, but left him in no doubt that I would apply to the judge if I didn't get what I believed to be satisfaction from him. I pointed out that in the manual he had shown me the day before, it made provision for every prisoner to get one free government letter every month. At that time that would have been around fifty-five free letters which he would have to provide, censor, and then post. I agreed with him that his men were not postmen, and told him to ask any one of them if they had ever had any bad words from me or if I showed them anything but respect.

I also pointed out that I paid for all my own letters and stamps and did not use any of the allotted government issue. In doing this I was giving him the wee idea that he could perhaps be making an extra few bob by claiming for stamps or letters that weren't being used. I made two copies using my own carbon paper and asked to see him the following morning.

In his office I presented him with my application and asked him to sign for it as well signing my own copy. He signed and told me to go back to my room. I wasn't in the room for long before the cell gate was opened and I was summoned back down to the office.

I could see that he was smiling very wryly, even if it wasn't showing on his face.

"How many letters do you want to send James Toner?" he asked, by this time smiling openly.

"Sir, I would be happy with three letters a week, I receive many and I think it is rude not to reply to them. I come from a faraway place and it is my means of keeping in touch with my friends and family back in Scotland".

"Ok James Toner, we don't need to file this application now then?" he was holding the letter in the air and almost pleading.

"No sir, you can put that in the bin if you so wish, but bear in mind I have got my copy which you signed and dated this morning".

I thanked him and returned to number six once more and felt that I had struck a blow for the prisoners. I hadn't of course. I had used their lack of literacy and their ignorance of the contents of the jail manual to further my own ends. I saw and still see no harm in that at all.

I was doing lots of reading, material I wouldn't have read before. Books about Moa, The Rise and Fall of the Third Reich, Gandhi`s 'Experiments with the Truth'. I read Viktor Frankl`s book about life in a Nazi concentration camp, 'Man's Search for Meaning'. From that book I drew incredible hope, he reasoned that if man had the "WHY" then they would always find the "HOW".

At the time I didn't realise it, but I was beginning to reprogramme myself, adjusting to the fact that I didn't know how long I would be in jail in India for, and not knowing what would be on the other end of it all for me. I stopped reading fiction; I had no need for it in the real world that I was living in at that time. Later in my time in jail I relaxed that rule though and read Shantaram, great read but too far-fetched to be true. I did though enjoy a wee read of some old Irvine Welsh classics, and even some of his stuff I hadn't read before like his collection of short stories titled 'Reheated Cabbage' and the hilariously dark 'Babylon Heights' which he co-wrote with Dean Cavanagh.

At the time I wasn't familiar with any of Dean's work, but after my release I came into contact with him through a social network site and now appreciate him for the genius that he is in his own right. Not just a jack of all trades but a master of many talents is Dean Cavanagh.

So I was keeping busy in the jail reading and writing, all the while waiting on my charge sheet being filed to see exactly what the evidence against me was going to be. I had learned how to write out applications to the various courts that the other less well-off prisoners were being tried in, so I became a sort of free legal aid application man. I was friendly with everyone and they were friendly with me in return. I said hello to everyone, but Bengre was still in his huff and I gave him plenty of opportunity to acknowledge me when I would look at him and smile, but he never took me up on it. The guy lived his life on the outside feeding off the fear of those unable to stand up to him, and he didn't come across as the type who could even have an argument with any of his mates without him being violent. His passing will not be mourned in many quarters when his day of reckoning does come. No problem, he was a proper cunt, but in the eyes of all the other prisoners

I was ok. I was the only westerner who integrated with the Indians in the jail, and that was no doubt one of the other things that made life easier for me than for most in Mapusa.

For the most part I managed to keep things in the day, didn't concern myself with the past, and definitely didn't think about the future, because at that point my future was directly connected with the day to day life I was living.

I was also reading about Taoism, Buddhism, Hinduism, and other forms of spirituality. I know Hinduism is a religion, but they have over 3 million Gods and believed in being reborn and at that point in time in Mapusa Jail in 2009 I would have read anything that helped me get through a difficult experience. Everything I read during that time was to lay the foundations for the man I have become today, I tried to put it all into practice back then too but it was not always easy.

Police telling you lies that your charge sheet would be ready in 3 or 4 months and your case would be finished in a year or a bit more didn't help. When you're told that, your mind sort of believes it, so when the 3 months passed then the 4 months, you start to get a bit uptight.

I was to be defended in my trial by Peter D` Souza, the best drug lawyer in Goa, but it would be the December of 2009 before I actually got to meet him. Up until that point we would only be seen by one of his understudies, my main point of contact would be Raju, the lawyer I had first met in Panjim Lock up when he was accompanied by the I.O in my case, P.S.I Punaji Gawas. It wasn't that I didn't trust Raju, I just wondered what his part in all this was to be honest.

Wee Tosh had been back over to visit me and brought me books and various other presents from the folks back home. Big Steevo and Leeann sent me Celtic tops, t-shirts, and other gifts. Four months in and I was coping well with my new found life and doing all I could to make things more comfortable for myself. I made an application to the judge to have some fruit and veg allowed at our weekly canteen. The only reason we were not originally allowed was that the guard who collected the lists and had to go to the markets to collect the canteen supplies was a lazy bastard.

I had asked to see the jail manual and found it made provision for us to be allowed to buy our own fruit and veg from our own money. It didn't help those who had no money who weren't in our cell, but those who had the money benefitted from my application when the judge ordered we be allowed essential vitamins and minerals we were being denied because of some lazy big Indian guard who was making money out of it anyway by making up his own prices as he went along. In the end we were allowed tomatoes, cucumber, mangoes, and other fruits.

In September 2009 just before the season began, there was the usual round up of visa overstay cases, mainly from the African countries of Nigeria and Kenya. Within the space of a week Mapusa had gone from this tiny overcrowded as it was wee jail, to this noisy even more crowded place with about another twenty more men on the numbers. All black, all big and strong, and all not giving a fuck because their lawyer would get them bail soon enough and they would be back out onto the streets in time for the season starting again in earnest.

To be honest, I loved watching the fear on the faces of the guards and the Indian prisoners alike. The Goan has his own version of the "N" word, that word is Hampri but none of them would have dared use it to their faces. All of these guys could speak English and they all love their football, so I flitted from group to group and spoke football with them. I wore the Celtic colours and they knew who my team was. They went by their made up English names like Monday, Friday, Beckham, and even James. It was much easier for us white guys to remember than Ngombe, Nfede, or whatever their actual given names were. They were mostly involved in the drug trade outside, and for some or indeed most, it was the common practice to get caught with 5 grams of cocaine for example, to be arrested then bailed and have their cases drag on for 5 years. It was all a big game to them and they were winning hands down on all fronts.

We would watch from our gate at lunch and dinner time when this line of six-foot-tall, 100 kilos of pure muscle guys looked at the amount of rice being dished out and they would cause uproar. The guards would be shitting themselves, as would poor Mungledas the outside caterer who brought the food into the jail. His portions were not the biggest and these guys took some feeding, pots were up in the air and plates were being thrown about, they kept their shows of dissent to their own native tongue so fuck knows what was being shouted, but the gist was they were not happy. Body language is international so wasn't hard to pick up on.

The noise these lads made speaking in their different dialogues and languages was deafening in the yard. I was going to write that may have been the sound at Rourke's Drift and I don't want to stand accused of being racist, but I'm saying it anyway.

If you were afraid of the black guys, you didn't go into the yard. I was no longer in the minority in that 25 foreigners who I could speak to had been parachuted in to Mapusa Beach and they had taken all the sunbeds away from the locals.

Then on the 30th October 2009 it all went pear shaped for me. After lunch that day one of the guards came round with a piece of paper. He began calling names out and telling people to get their gear together, the names being called out were on the transfer list. This was my first experience of this process but I took an instant dislike to it.

"James Toner, get your bed and clothes together, you are being transferred to Vasco." One of the guards shouted in to my cell.

I was in shock. I didn't want to be transferred to a prison an hour and a half away from Mapusa. My court was in Mapusa, I could walk to and from it in ten minutes, but it would take an hour and a half to drive from Vasco. It would take even longer in the old ramshackle bus that they used to escort prisoners from the outlying jails to the courts in Mapusa, Panjim, and Margoa.

I sat down and looked at the guard. "I`m not going to Vasco." I told him.

"You have to do what you are told to do, James Toner, and the order has your name on it, get your things ready, the bus is outside."

I could see out of the corners of my eyes the other people in the cell who had been ordered to pack getting their things in order. I could also see the look of relief on the faces those who had been spared the axe, so to speak.

You see, Vasco Sada Jail was more than the wee place I had been kept prisoner in Mapusa since my remand there. It was known for its gang fights and was always in the papers for this violent action or that being perpetrated on staff or by inmate on inmate. I wanted none of that and told the guard to go and fuck off.

He did and soon came back with the small jailer, he was called that because he was the younger of the two in charge and his voice hadn't broken yet.

He asked me why I was creating a problem, I told him the problem was not of my making and asked him why they hadn't just put the last lot of overstay inmates on the Vasco bus. I understood the problem of overcrowding more than he did and told him so.

He threatened to call the local police station and that is exactly what he did, next thing I know there are four policemen walking towards my cell. One who was very obviously in charge, and the other three who were all carrying weapons. By weapons I mean guns and not your normal Indian police weapon which is a bamboo stick.

The P.S.I who was in charge asked me what the problem was. I told him I was being transferred and was refusing to go. It didn't make any sense moving the drug cases to a prison over 60 km away from the court they would be appearing in once every two weeks at least until the charge sheet arrived.

His advice to me was to go along with the transfer and to put in a request for a transfer back when I got to Vasco. He made that part sound very easy, but in reality it wasn't at all.

Then he paid me the compliment of telling me he thought I was an intelligent man, which was only to mask his own threat that we could do this the easy way or the hard way. It was my choice.

I picked up my belongings and trudged down the office to check out of Mapusa judicial lock up, I thought it would be for the last time, but I would be back only not for a wee while yet. The young jailer even tried to explain himself to me, telling me the only reason we were all being sent to Vasco was because none of us caused any trouble. A back handed compliment landing us a sort of perverse reward, we parted with a shake of the hand but I could feel his fear. People who have fear and are given positions of power can be dangerous, and I can see this wee bastard being a thorn in a few people's sides during his career in the Goan Prison Service. With that I made my way outside to the bus that had been waiting on me sorting things out.

Postscript:

As you have probably gathered, I saw Ashpak Bengre as one of the evilest cunts I have ever met. He thrived on instilling fear in other people, and killing and maiming were second nature to him. It really came as no surprise to me when I read that he'd been murdered in Colvale Jail. I certainly didnae shed a single tear, though there may have been a wee smile. It was an inevitable conclusion to a life of violence...

Chapter 12: Vasco Sada Jail

There were 2 buses that transferred 20 of us that Friday morning, and I could tell that some of these lads were shiteing themselves about being sent to Vasco. Paranoia is said to be contagious, so I soon felt the same way about this unknown but well publicised hellhole we were all about to be put into.

We arrived at Vasco in the early evening after dinner had already been given out in the jail, but the processing of us 20 newcomers took more than a few hours so we missed the dinner until later on when we got ours, nice and cold.

The full thing about Vasco was it was a proper prison; I had been locked up for 5 months but in a small jail, not unlike the old cowboy movies (think Hannibal Hayes and Kid Curry if you can/will). This was more like the jail I`d expected to be have been put in back in May when I was arrested.

This was a big jail that looked to me as if it was 100 years old, turned out it had been built less than fifteen years previously.

They trooped the 20 of us into a space outside the main office, and one by one they began to do the administration work required to induct us into the jail. As I said before, I could feel the fear but now I was hearing it and I could even smell it in the air.

"Let's make sure we stick together in here." I heard.

I had to laugh at that one because the people who had been transferred would not have been looking out for one another in Mapusa. There were a couple of little pockets of pairs or threes who always stayed together, but mostly in Mapusa it was every man for himself.

This convict came along with bedding and our new steel plates and cups. I knew he was a convict because of the clothes he was wearing. His blue short trousers were the bottom half of a uniform that included a white shirt. I say white but this guy`s had long since ceased to be that colour. He had the look of a sex case about him, I don't know why I thought that but it was the feeling I got off him straight away. As it turned out I was not wrong.

He gave out these wee piles of old blankets, sheets, and towels, along with bashed and filthy plates and cups. I looked at him and told him to go back to the store and get me new gear. He said he couldn't and that was all that was in the store, I once again stared straight through him, and told him I wasn't asking, I was telling him, and I wasn't going to stand about all day until he had served all the Indians. He hurried away and came back with newer cup, plate, and bedding for me. They were still not the best but better than before I suppose. I never got to find out his name and never really saw him speaking to anyone in my time in Vasco, but he was in for a rape case and had been convicted.

I was one of the foreign crew but we had already been pre-warned, by one of the other inmates, that we would all be split up once in Vasco. But I got on with most folk anyhow so it didn't really matter to me where I went, I was just genuinely worried about being in mainstream prison now. This was it, the real deal.

I think I can say without fear of contradiction that there are many tougher and harder men than myself who would not have lasted 2 minutes in either Mapusa or Vasco. It wasn't about being hard or tough, I'm neither. It was about using your brain and not getting involved in any jail shit that was nothing to do with you.

The process of registration seemed to go on for hours and finally it was over, we were allocated a trustee who basically, and I'm being honest while smiling here, looked after the foreigners, and gathered 5 of us together. You're coming to room number 7, my room, he said with pride. His name was Anan Kumbli, his alleged crime was murder. He had allegedly been in a relationship with some English wummin who had given him money to open a beach shack cum bar and it all went pear shaped, as it always does. He had been charged with murder by stabbing the lady to death and cutting her throat.

We picked up our blankets and other possessions and headed towards room number 7 while this fella led the way.

He looked as proud as punch when he brought us into the room, they would have known we were coming and they would have been glad to get the foreign contingent. They assumed that we had money or access to money, and that we would only bring or give the room an "economic boost". They were right, I always had money for my canteen thanks to wee Tosh flying over when I was first arrested and leaving an English bloke a couple of quid to make sure I had all the things that I needed to make life more comfortable in the environment I was going to be living in for the next 15/18 months, at least we had been told that by my defence team.

I was housed in number seven with the two Russians, Viktor and Vashya. The Arab David and Milanac who had been so close to Bengre but now found himself detached because he was left behind in Mapusa.

The new room was much bigger than the one we had left in Mapusa, and we were all allocated our spaces on the floor while the occupants made us feel welcome. Some did it out of kindness I'm sure, but they were once again mostly sharks circling, hoping to catch the smell of blood so they could move in for the kill.

All in all, the boys in the cell made us very welcome that night and produced grass and pills which they readily shared with the newcomers. Like I have said before it's the jail, it's your time, so you do with it as you see fit, and if the odd pill is what makes it easier for you then the odd pill it is. I had my piece of Charas to bring to the party, so I'd have been marked down at an early point as someone who could get shit and who, more importantly, could get the money to buy the nice sweet piece of Charas I shared with them that first night.

They wanted to know about Mapusa. Who ran the jail? Was it Ashpak? Because he was an enemy of each and every one of them in the room that night, all except maybe Viktor the Russian. Bengre had done him no wrong so he had no grievance with him. Nothing wrong with that system I'd say. Someone mentioned him not being my friend and I explained the situation with him, we had got on ok, but all his friendships were based on fear, intimidation, and him controlling the relationship. I wasn't his enemy as such, but we didn't speak to one another anymore. His choice I explained, I have no problem with anyone and don't expect that I'll have any in here. I just wanted my case to finish so I could go home and I wasn't interested in any bother with anyone. I told them I didn't take tobacco in my bong and they sent them my way all night.

There was definitely an element of more freedom in Vasco that I could feel from the very start. It unquestionably stemmed from the fact that the staff were all corrupt and had no control in the jail. As soon as that guard takes the first bribe he`s in for the full nine yards. No getting out for them, and to be honest if you were on £60 a month you'd be taking the bribe as well. We didn't know it at the time, but you could get anything in Vasco and I mean anything.

That first night I was so stoned I fell asleep in another man's spot – an act which is normally taboo - and in the morning, he got moved because I 'seemed to sleep quite well in the spot I had taken'. Nothing to do with the fact that I was to be kept happy by all means possible, and they did go out of their way to make me feel as well as one can feel in jail in another country, a third world developing nation but with a penal system that is both backward and laughable.

This cell, number 7, was different from Mapusa too in that there were people from all over India and in for all sorts of different crimes.

The boss man of Vasco was in number 7, his name was Mario Fernandez, and he was on remand for murder. Allegedly he had stabbed some ex-girlfriend to death and had been on remand for 3 years when I first met him. He couldn't have been any nicer to me and was always the first on the scene if I had any problems with guards; these were generally caused by the communications barrier which Mario always sorted. We got on well from the start, but he was just another Ashpak Bengre, only he had this different approach which I found more menacing. Mario had killed his ex-girlfriend, stabbed her multiple times and ran this room. Would that have been the case in a Scottish Jail? I don't think so. Vasco was going to take a wee bit of settling into, I could feel that. As it happened, Ashpak and Mario were also sworn enemies and they had been part of the gang feuds that had plagued Vasco over the years. Bengre had been transferred from Vasco to Mapusa after their last altercation, and Mario did not hide his hatred or contempt for the other murderer.

Vasco had a totally different regime from Mapusa. It had more order and a sort of structure which began at 6 every single morning when the guards came to your cell and rattled the bars to waken you up. You then had to line up sitting in rows on the floor while the guards counted you. Then if you so pleased, you could go back to your slumber and sleep till whenever you liked. At 7, the tea was served downstairs at the dinner hatch, and again it consisted of 2 bread rolls and a cup of sugary tea.

One Flew Over the Cuckoo's Nest springs to mind at the sight of all these half-asleep walking dummies all heading downstairs for their sugary tea and their 2 dry bread rolls. In the cells the rolls generally had jam or butter or biscuits put on them to make it feel like we did have a breakfast after all. This had a bad effect on my stomach, and I was sick each and every day I was in Vasco Sub Jail Sada. There was far too much spice and far too much sugar too. Heartburn always led to the acid refluxing and me being sick every day I was there. I don't suppose it helped our kidneys and liver that we had to drink local water too. I had some prostate gland trouble while inside which has now manifested itself to some sore kidneys, infections no less.

It wasn't long before I was assigned my own "steward" In Vasco, in American jails he might have been called "Ma

Biatch". His name was Matthew Gomes and our relationship worked like this; he washed my clothes and cup and plate and took my turn at cleaning the room when it was my shot. In return I bought him a few things from the canteen and shared most of anything I had with him. He had the nickname Churchill because he was always claiming to be the friend of the Goan Politician, Churchill Alamoa, and telling everyone that Churchill would get him out of this mess.

What was 57-year-old Mathew Churchill Gomes`s mess? He was in for rape and allowed to mix with the general population. The thing about Churchill was I didn't get the same feeling off him as I did from the other rape cases in Vasco, and there were many of them. I asked him to show me his charge sheet.

He brought the charge sheet back and sat beside me while I read it. It began with a medical report that showed the tests carried out on both him and the alleged victim. It stated that both he and the 35-38-year-old wummin had both shown signs of having sex in the 24 hours previous to the test being carried out. Neither of them had cleaned themselves since the sex act took place.

The charge sheet also carries out a psychological assessment of them both which placed them both in the lower regions in terms of the IQ test they undertook. Churchill was in the high 50s, and the lady was lower than that in the 40s. I told him that the sheet showed that they had had sex; he said it was only oral. I asked him what he meant and he said he`d kissed her breasts and she had given him a blow job, that is my term and not the one he used. He used the term oral sex to cover a variety of acts so I`m not sure what he meant by it.

The lady was a housekeeper at Churchill's place, and I have no doubt that the two of them had sex. She stayed out all night, and when she went home to the house she lived in with her Aunt, she was questioned about her whereabouts. The lady with the IQ of a child panicked and told her Aunt that Churchill had forced himself on her; the Aunt being a little old Goan Catholic felt the shame of her niece and called the police. They immediately went and arrested him and he had been in Vasco for the previous six months. I could be wrong of course, but I don't believe Churchill raped the wummin. They had sex, and some fucking backward holier than thou old dried up Roman fuckin Catholic turned it into something it never was and ruined that cunt's life.

He looked after me in my time at Vasco and I made sure he was ok too. Clothes all spotless and I couldn't even go for a cup of tea but he ran down the stairs and got it for me. I played football most afternoons in Vasco, and no sooner had I taken my wet kit off than Churchill had it steeping in a bucket of water and soap powder making sure it was ready for the next day's play. I would wake up every morning to a small pile of freshly washed clothes at the bottom of my bed. One time he even took one for me from the Governor of the jail. There had been a raid and a mobile phone was found under a young lad's pillow. He hadn't put it there; it was that Arab once again. The young boy was slapped and beaten in front of us, and it took all my self-restraint and knowledge it was none of my business to stay out of it. He got punched and kicked and led away downstairs for the rest of his punishment I can only imagine. I had a SIM card which Churchill looked after for me. He wasn't a sharp tool remember.

I went to court in the afternoon with the Arab, and when we came back we were called into the Governor's office. The young local lad stood in tears and could not look at me. The Governor told me that the lad had told him the phone was mine and I was in trouble. I told him that the lad was telling lies and he had better tell the truth, I knew it was not his phone. Next thing the Arab has been brought in and he had also been crying, for goodness sake I thought. They are just going to blame this phone on me. Lots of talk in foreign tongues ensued and I could hear Churchill's name being mentioned, I knew he would break down and tell them straight away if questioned, and I was very angry with both the Arab and the young lad. They had both stuck me in for sure, but Churchill would be the icing on the cake.

Churchill came upstairs and entered the office of the Governor and was immediately quizzed about the phone. He did the usual thing and began crying like he had lost his play piece. Churchill though, unknown to me, was taking every bit of blame from me and putting it at someone else's door. He admitted using the phone, but didn't know who it belonged too and told the Governor that he had used it because all the other prisoners had been kidding him on that Mahanon Naik - a serial killer who had been accused of killing eighteen women - was going to get him next. Mahanon Naik is another name to Google if you care to find out about this paradise that is Goa. Well the result was the Governor told me to leave the room and get back to my cell. Churchill had proved he stood where younger harder men than him had not.

Not long after I was to leave Vasco myself, Churchill did too, I went back to Mapusa though, but he was found guilty and sentenced to seven years in Aguada Jail. I have no doubt he was innocent, but the lack of funds to pay for a decent lawyer coupled with the fact he was daft, mentally challenged, or whatever the fuckin politically correct name for it is, meant that he was always going to be found guilty. At the time I am writing this, he will be half way through his seven-year term for a crime he most definitely DID NOT commit. Mathew Gomes was just one of the many who couldn't speak for himself and couldn't afford decent legal representation and he was always going to be found guilty, it is all just a big numbers game after all.

The main problem with Vasco for me was that the gates opened at 6 in the morning and closed again at ten, we were then locked up for four hours before being opened for another four in the afternoon between two o clock and six at night. We weren't allowed outside during that time but the section or our landing was open to everyone. To most of the prisoners in Vasco this was brilliant, but to me it was a right pain in the arse. There was no peace, no solitude, or at times even space to gather your thoughts. I never liked that idea from the first morning in the place, and it only got worse for me as the time there went on. So basically from six in the morning people were up milling about, and soon the place started buzzing with people from other cells in yours and all these making far too much noise in about eight different Indian languages.

Indians have some very strange toilet habits first thing in the morning, and they all made some racket while carrying out their ablutions, a word which at one time I didn't think actually existed. They began each day by emptying their bowels, having a shit like. That was of course followed by the actual practice of wiping their backsides with their bare hands, or the left hand to be exact. A cold bath then followed before the horrendous process of the teeth, tongue, and fucking tonsils being brushed. Try putting a toothbrush down your throat and brushing it; unless you have the gag reflex of Linda Lovelace you are almost making yourself sick. That was the idea of it as it happens; the Hindu purges all the dirt out of their body before they light the incense sticks and start praying to whichever of the three million Gods they called their own.

All of this was done in an actual toilet block which was in the middle of all the cells, so it was very hard not to hear all that was going on. I also have this thing about people walking about with their toothbrush in their mouths outside the toilet, white paste surrounding the mouth as they try to speak to you. I often had to turn my head away while pointing an outstretched hand in the opposite direction because some Indian wanted to chat while cleaning his throat, teeth, and tongue. Get tae fuck.

The actual toilet block was something I hope never to see again in my life, anywhere. It had one entrance to it and then formed a sort of C shape. Along one side of the C were three cubicles that served as showers, again the concept of a shower or a bath in an Indian Jail is a tap about three feet off the floor from which flowed freezing cold water at set times during the day.

Along the other side of the C shape were three Indian Style toilets, holes in the ground to me and you. The walls were tiled and kept clean, but the smell that came from the hole in the ground made using the toilet a very unpleasant experience altogether. Then of course you had to get used to the left-hand thing and us in the West don't like touching shite, it's dirty isn't it. As I have already stated, I am now fully converted to the principle that soap and water cleans your bum a hell of a lot better than paper ever could.

That's right we do that, but we treat our bottoms differently, we clean our arses using paper. My time in jail in

India taught me that soap and water is what you need to clean your backside, and not Andrex or any other 4 ply mega product that is mass produced for the consumer market. I can't be sure, because I haven't googled it, but I would hazard a guess that toilet paper is a product that was gradually introduced onto the shopping lists by the big companies over the years by using the hygiene argument. It's not that important to get the facts right about that because I'm only making an observation as I said. Shoot me down if you like, but you're missing the point of the story if your googling my wee toilet facts.

One of the worst parts of going to the toilet was that to get to the shower or to the hole in the ground you had to wade through this big puddle of waste from the sinks that the prisoners used to clean their teeth, their plates after dinner or whatever else they spat into them. Your feet were dry when you went in but soaking when you came back out. Everybody sported a sort of trench foot disease, the fungi caused by continually having to plough through the waste to get to the other facilities; it was a very unpleasant experience and one that everyone had to endure. It was even worse still if you happened to slip and land in the big fucking stinking puddle, I saw that happening more than once in my time in Vasco. Never tae me but eh.

I now also believe that squatting is the healthy way to do the toilet as well, but we in the west know different though.

Gandhi was once asked the question: What did he think of civilization in the west? He replied that "he thought it would be a great idea". I now believe that it goes both ways.

Viktor was hilarious with them in the morning, he used to throw cups and books or whatever came to hand at the noise makers and they`d scuttle away to make their racket elsewhere. He was right next to me so I didn't mind him chasing all these bums away, but me and Viktor soon had our own wee fall out which resulted in him moving along one and Vashya , the other Russian, moving into Viktors space. It all came about because during daytime the done thing was to roll your bedding up and give the room the look of having more space. It also meant no one was sitting on their bed eating their dinners which just attracted ants by the thousand. The problem was Viktor was a big lazy bastard and not exactly very clean either. He owned two pair of shorts and two ripped t-shirts. He even went to court in his shorts and t-shirt. He called it jungle style, I know what I called him, and I`ll allow you all to make your minds up about him and his habits. He was a big smelly bastard. The three of us all slept in a wee line but in the end up I came back to the room one day and Viktor had moved along one leaving Vashya in between us. Apparently it was my incessant moaning that caused him to move along one. Now I just leaned over Vasha's shoulder and moaned safe in the knowledge that he wasn't leading an army of ants onto my bed that night. My memories of Viktor are fond ones. He was another good cunt.

The guy who had “found” us on the day of our admission and brought us all into number seven, Anan, was a bit of a strange character but he had been on remand for some time, was the jail pass-man and medicine man as well. He dealt with the prisoner’s canteen requests, and when the doctor came round once a week he would deal with the prescriptions that the doctor dished out. He had no problem adding things to your prescription or altering the number of pills that the jail doctor had prescribed. He made sure that if anything was required to aid sleep then it was always available, he could sort out your cough for you most of the time as well. The man with access to codeine and sleeping pills in your cell is as valuable as the man who has the seemingly constant supply of Charas. We got on alright.

He was a right weird cat if truth be told, and he was preparing himself for the worst case scenario which in his case would have been life in Aguada. He had found God and went through this full big show of lighting candles and praying at the same time every evening before we had our dinner, I`m not knocking it I`m simply saying. I think he knew it was not going to go his way in the trial, and he had admitted to us all that he did kill the wummin in any case, none of my business was my policy remember so I did just that. I minded my own business.

Vasco was sort of split into four different types of alleged offenders. The foreigners and the Nepalis were all drug cases. The Indian were split into murderers, thieves, and sex cases. There is an average of one murder a week in the paradise that is Goa, and twice as many reported rapes. Theft is committed on a daily basis in Goa, bikes, phones, and anything that the opportunist thief can lay his hands on. So Vasco had a varying degree of alleged criminal in its ranks, and they were all allowed to mix freely. Remember this, I come from a society where certain crimes are not tolerated by the other criminals in the system, but what I had to also bear in mind was that each and every one of those people was claiming innocence and I was one of them. I just had to learn to live in among people who I would not have associated with on the outside, but that didn't mean I had to be their friends while I was in jail with them.

Chapter 13: James Toner James Toner James Fuckin Toner

I should perhaps attempt to explain the law under which I'm being charged and the process which an accused has to go through while waiting for the trial to begin, and then the torture the accused suffers when it does begin. At the time of me writing this chapter, it has been 39 months since my arrest, almost 12 of which I spent in custody.

I was arrested and charged under section 20(c)iii of the Narcotic Substance and Psychotropic Substance (N.D.P.S) act of 1984. Until then India had no drug laws. I was held in police custody for 7 days to allow for further investigation, and at the end of the 7 days I was produced in front of a judge who remanded me to 14 days' judicial custody, or JC as it is more commonly known.

The accused then goes to jail for 14 days, and at the end of that period, he/she is then produced again in front of the judge and remanded for a further 14 days. The reason for this is that Indian law regarding the NDPS act states that a person must be shown to the judge every 14 days until the actual trial begins.

The trial proper won't begin for at least 6 months, when the report from the chemical analyst who has examined whatever the accused has been charged with being in possession of has been tested and proven to be what the police say it is, in my case Charas. The 6-month rule only applies to Charas, and anyone waiting on a report for being in possession of any chemical substance usually has to wait 12 months. The actual law states 6 months, but for chemicals they allow applications for 60 day extensions which will be given up until 12 months have passed.

So for the first 4 months of me being in custody I knew that nothing was going to move in my case, and the day out every fortnight was just that, a day out. In my case I spent the first 5 months in Mapusa JC before my enforced transfer to Vasco Jail. After 4 months you start to believe the police when they tell you that your report will be ready next time and your case will begin.

Police the world over are lying bastards, they tell lies every time they enter the witness box, that is only my opinion, but I know from experience that my opinion is not far off being the truth. In my own case, I had been moved to Vasco when in the last few days of my 6 months I was taken to court and given my charge sheet. That is the first time that the accused has any idea of the case against him or what the witness are saying about the case.

The charge sheet consists of an initial report stating why the police arrested me and then the evidence of the main witness, the Investigating Officer (I.O). In my case, P.S.I Punaji Gawas. He was the one who compiled the report which states the charge against you. All the other witnesses in the case merely sign copied sheets of the I.O's evidence claiming what they have said is the truth, and I do mean exact copies. So what you have is one copper telling the big lie, and the rest of them telling the even bigger lie that he is in fact telling the truth.

There is one independent expert who has examined the substance to prove what it actually is, and 2 other independent witnesses who are supposed to have been asked beforehand to accompany the police on the raid to arrest the accused, in this case me. These witnesses are called Panch witnesses and are never really present at the scene of any of the arrests. They are actually trained in their evidence later before they are brought to court to give their statement in front of the judge.

There is also a senior police officer who has allegedly given permission for the raid to take place and who also takes the stand to state as such.

The lower ranked police officers give their evidence first before the Panch gives his or hers. Then the stand is taken by the senior police officer who gave the permission for the raid, followed by the last witness, the I.O. He is the one who has written the statement that all the other officers and the Panch witness have sworn in court to be the truth. He merely answers questions that the Prosecutor asks him, then is cross examined by the defence lawyer. I don't possibly see how a system like that can be called Justice.

Please bear with me through this wee part, because I'm just trying to show how farcical this system is and the difference between Western and Indian law.

At the end of the prosecutions part in the trial, the defence is allowed to make a statement. Not call any witnesses, but they can make a statement basically denying everything that has been put in front of the court.

There then follows the argument between the prosecutor and the defence counsel.

Another date is then set for the judge to make their decision as to the guilt or innocence of the accused party. If the decision is guilty there is then another date called Point of Sentence, where the judge gives the accused who is now the guilty party his or her time in jail. In my case that will be at least ten years without parole and a fine of £3000, which turns into another year if the person who has been given the ten years can't pay the extra bounty.

So if you can try to imagine a jail full of men who are waiting to see exactly what's been said about their cases and some having to wait at least a year. Tensions ran high as the Indians like to say. "Don't take tension" is a phrase I wouldn't mind if I never heard it again in my whole life.

Then the time comes for the accused to be given his charge sheet, and I can swear that I read about 20 of them and all that had been changed was dates, places, and the person.

The rest was exactly the same as the next guy's, and I kid you not about that.

You are given your sheet then produced in front of the same judge who has seen you for the past 6 months and asked:

"How do you plead to the charge?"

"Not guilty, your honour." I said.

With that, I was taken back to Vasco for all the "jail lawyers" to have a look at my chances of freedom or if I was getting the big ten. The first thing I noticed about mine was that it had been ready for 3 months, sitting on some desk waiting till they had dragged the 6 months out before producing it in court.

I know at this point there will be some of you who still don't get why I was framed, set up by the Anti-Narcotic Cell of the Goan Police. Some of you who will be thinking it's all made up and I'm guilty as sin, please read on then because you will enjoy the part at the end where the noose is placed round my neck but I'm saved in the nick of time when the Queen and Daniel Craig bungee jump from a hovering "strong" helicopter and pluck me to safety. I`m sitting here smiling, I hope you are too.

Sorry, if you bear in mind what I have just told you about the system and how it is supposed to work, it's all based on corruption and that corruption goes from the top of the government of India right down to the guy who collects the fares on the buses. I`ll use my own case as an example of how it all fits into place in the big jigsaw that it is. I believe it's very difficult to live an incorrupt life in a country that positively invites everyone to be corrupt.

I`m admitting to have been in Anjuna on the 23 May 2009 - to you the reader that is - and I was there to buy a quantity of Charas. I was going to sort out 3 kilos for an associate in Colva, and get a nice piece that would last a few of us over the monsoon until the fresh stuff came down from the mountains in the new season. I did go to the home of a young Goan called Omkar Mahalaxsmi. I had known him and his family and friends for a number of years.

I left his house as I have said before, with the carrier bag which I placed under the seat and my own 400 grams of Charas. The taxi travelled south for 15 minutes before it was stopped in the middle of the main highway at about one in the afternoon 10 miles from Mahalaxmi`s home on the busy road between Goa and Bombay, like the A1, the driver slowed to a stop to go over a big speed breaker. At that point I realised that I had been set up by Omkar Mahalaxsmi and I was about to be arrested. In the space of a minute they had me from the taxi into the back and the driver in another car and then we were gone.

I was to meet the driver again soon in the main police station in Panjim. He was sat down on a chair next to mine and he was breaking his heart. A 50-year-old man crying his eyes out because of one little £12 taxi job and I felt bad about it.

"He was only driving the taxi, sir." I pled with the policeman.

"How do we know he is not part of this gang of yours, James Toner?"

That was the first mention of any gang and I just thought it was funny, too funny as it turns out.

They spoke to the driver in Konkani, the local Goan tongue. He was obviously telling them what had happened and I don't blame him, because as I was to learn it would not have been uncommon for him to end up as my co-accused.

The driver would have thought he`d won a watch with the big job as well, bit like an airport job for a taxi driver from one of the schemes in Glasgow. I`m not sure, but I think they kept him for about 5 or 6 hours before they let him go, we didn't get the chance to say good bye.

I don't deny that I was committing a crime in another country, and for that I deserved anything that the laws of that country deemed fit. What I am saying, and I haven't stopped saying it since I was freed, is that I was NOT at Chapora bus stand on the 23rd May 2009, or on any other day for that matter. I have never been to the scene of my alleged arrest, and would swear to that on my death bed. The full case scenario was made up.

Manufactured to cover up what was actually happening in Goa at that time, the full Anti Narcotic Cell was rotten and corrupt to the core, but their time would come and I was there to be part of that as well. Or are they part of my experience? I don't know, but it is both me and the ANC and our stories are intrinsically linked in any case.

That is what happened to me the day I was arrested. The report filling was all done in the police station later in that week, and I watched a lot of it being done. I just didn't get what was happening; it was all to become apparent soon though.

Bearing in mind the way I have described my actual arrest, and that is the way it happened, this is how it was described in my charge sheet and was signed by 18 people as being the truth and nothing but the truth.

"Acting on specific and reliable information that one foreign national, a Scotsman by the name of James Toner would be approaching Chapora bus stand with a bag of drugs. The intended buyer for the drugs was at that point unknown. The suspect would be wearing green khaki shorts and a green t-shirt. He was around 5feet 6 inches and medium build. The raiding party hid in various points in the location of the bus stand and waited on the suspect coming along. At roughly 3o'clock, one male was seen arriving at the spot and the I.O cautioned his men that they thought that this was the suspect."

“The police officers approached the man and identified themselves as ANC, and told the suspect, James Toner, that they suspected him to be in the possession of a controlled drug, namely Charas. They then offered the accused the opportunity to search them before they commenced the search of his person. James Toner declined the offer to search the policemen and was asked to hand over the grey shoulder bag he was carrying. He did so and on opening the bag the contents were seen to be a white plastic bag. They opened that bag and I.O Punaji Gawas smelled the substance before announcing that it was indeed Charas”.

According to the report there then followed a 3-hour process were the Charas was weighed and then sealed before being sent to the Office of the ANC. It would then be sent to the office of the chemical analyst who had an office just outside Panjim, about half an hour away from the police HQ. Every single bit of their case was lies. Why the fuck would they need to do that when I had been caught bang to rights so to speak.

Bearing in mind this is the official version, I was then taken back to Panjim police HQ before being taken down to my have my flat in Colva searched. According to the official version, I had refused to answer any of their questions about the bag, its contents, or where I’d got it from or who I had intended to sell it to. That part is true because I didn’t answer any questions, partly because they didn’t` ask me any questions.

At the time that struck me as being a bit weird, but with time and the benefit of hindsight they didn`t need to ask me any questions. They were going to come up with their own version of events so why question me about the day's going on. As my story progresses it will become even more obvious as to why there was no need to ask me anything about the Charas, it belonged to them all along but that didn't come out until months later.

Anyway I got back to Vasco with my charge sheet and I can laugh at it now, but it was the highlight of the week for the lags in Vasco Sada Jail where I was now housed. Every jail has its pseudo lawyers and this one was no different, so after I managed to get a look at it myself, my charge sheet was passed round so all the Ironsides and the Petrocellis could have a good look at it. These bastards, as I was to find out, just loved to tell someone that their charge sheet was watertight and they most likely would be found guilty.

The guilty/not guilty system here works on a points scheme. The prosecution tries to get as many points as he can and the defence tries to get the points to cast doubt upon your guilt. So the jail lawyers all passed my charge sheet round and talked amongst themselves about the fact that my sheet seemed to be particularly tight, not leaving much room for me to escape the ten-year sentence that awaited me and still hangs over me like a big dark rain cloud if I am found guilty.

No one told me that though. I had to hear that from someone who had heard it from someone else, so I could then go back to the source and see what the problem with my tight charge sheet was.

Ironside, or whichever jail lawyer had made the ten-year decision, would then just say that in all the charge sheets they looked at there was always some mistake whether clerical or legal, but mine appeared to have none. Tight as the proverbial duck's backside so to speak, if you know what I mean. I`m sure most of these arseholes actually took great pleasure in telling some poor condemned soul- that day it was me- that they were doomed. That they had no chance of getting out of this and definitely faced ten years.

So now you have your charge sheet, you have been formally charged in court and your trial has begun, even though nothing has actually happened yet as such. You have been given your next date for court, but now you were in another category and you didn't have to be presented in court every two weeks. I had been told by Milana that the process was in three parts a long time ago when I was first arrested. The part waiting on your charge sheet when you simply went to court every two weeks and came back knowing you'd be back again in another two weeks. That part of the process was tedious at first, but you soon became accustomed to the wee day out every two weeks, good gear on and sitting in the back of a crowded bus sweating like a bad smuggler waiting to be told to come back again in two weeks. You actually came to look forward to that part when you put the good going ashore clothes on and went out on the town, albeit it with a two man police escort. As the time grew nearer for the charge sheet to be ready, you did feel a wee pang of excitement that today might be the day you get the sheet and the real shit would be about to begin.

I had also been pretty fortunate that the day before I arrived at Vasco there had been another British prisoner added to the numbers. His name was Danny (Ajay) Kaushal, half-Indian, but from Manchester and 120 kilograms of solid muscle at least. Him being British and us both holding the same passport lent a wee bit of added support to my side of the foreigners' ranks.

All the Indians assumed we must have known one another, and as it happens he was arrested in Colva where my flat at the time was. His mate had died in his room, the police had conducted a check on big Danny`s passport, and they discovered he was wanted in the UK after being given a 15-year sentence in his absence on a violent kidnapping charge. I believe that he was a big dangerous man if he were to be crossed, but me and AJ, that was his Indian and his jail name, got on really well from the off. There exists an extradition treaty between Britain and India, and he was waiting on the British police coming to collect him.

We spoke on our first morning in the yard together.

"What's the chances of escaping from here Jim?" He asked.

"Every chance Danny, (which was his English and Colva known name) you just have to settle in here and take things easy, then it will be possible for a price to get you picked up at a medical and you could vanish. Your colour and the fact you speak Hindi have to go in your favour, I`d think mate. The secret is just being the cuddly big bear, don't fight them because they are frightened of you as it is, and after a while they will relax and only 2 guards will take you to the hospital. They won't even give chase."

We walked together most days and he was definitely in no hurry to go back to the UK to face a 15-year sentence for his violent crime. But Danny was so hot headed that in his first week he had knocked out the Colva Police Inspector who had arrested him and attacked an assistant governor in the jail by punching him and spitting in his face, so that made the idea of an escape a hell of a lot more difficult for him to carry out. Instead of 2 escorts he had ten, and they tied him with rope like a fuckin bear when they were taking him to court or to any medical appointments.

Totally inhumane, and I'm saying this now that Miss Shilpa Caldiera, the British Consul here in Goa, knew about the treatment Danny was getting and she knew he was being tied with ropes going out of the jail, but she did nothing to stop this clear breach of human rights.

I settled right into the way of life in Vasco and became a bit of a hero amongst the other lads, because at 44 I was still down in the yard playing football with the younger boys and more than holding my own. Running about moaning, pointing, and shouting like fuck in my Scottish accent. No-one understood one word of it which might not have been a bad thing. We started games between landings, and in my 3 and half months there, we were never beaten. The football matches were like nothing else I had experienced in a lifetime of playing grassroots football. For a start, the rules were a bit ambiguous in that whatever Mario decided was generally how it went. Add to that mix the fact that Mario was running around like a madman having taken half a dozen Nitrazepam sleeping tablets. You might be thinking he`d have just gone to sleep, and that would have been the case had he at any point laid down, but Mario was fighting the sleeping urge in the same way Temazapam(Jellies) takers did in the 1980s and 90s before they were banned. Not many of the players actually had footwear either, so they were running around on their bare feet taking lumps out of toes and soles because we weren't playing at Wembley either remember.

Some were lucky to have one shoe, which would be sort of bandaged because the sole was hanging off, and I saw a few arguments in the run up to the matches with two lads arguing over the left or the right shoe as well. Fantastic memories that I can reach out and touch right now; the smell of stale sweat off the boy who would be serving you dinner later in the day while wearing the same clothes he had during our daily battle. Me? I would have looked resplendent in whichever Celtic strip I wore, and wearing the Reebok running shoes that came down the back of legs or crunched the toes of many willing opponents. They kicked and fully expected to get kicked back by me. I stood on toes and pulled hairs from legs too though, none of these lads learned to play football on the Glenwood Hockey pitch in Castlemilk, Glasgow. I did.

It was during my second month in Vasco that my mum and son came over from Scotland to visit me. Not to forget Ashley McDonald, my friend's daughter who is like a niece to me as well. The first visit was a strange and tense one for me. I had been building myself up for this visit for months, and when it did come it was horrible.

To sit in that small room with my mum and son and someone else who loved me was such a strange experience. They are looking round because they want to see the surroundings I'm living in, and it's all very emotional as you can imagine, although there were no tears at that first visit. To get to touch my son and give him a big cuddle and to look at the pain in my mum's eyes and etched on her face was torture for me. I explained to my son that I was not a bad man. I hadn`t killed or raped or stolen off an old lady, I'd made a bad choice and that's why I was there.

He just looked at me and told me he knew I wasn't a bad guy but I was stupid to end up in there.

In the two weeks that followed they visited me another three times, two of which had been specially arranged by my lawyers' understudy, Raju. They became more relaxed, and to this day Ashley I'm in your debt for the risk you took for me, when some couldn't even lift a pen, big respect for that Ashley. Bigger balls than most men I know in terms of being so brave (Daft). Only kidding Ashley, I loved you before but that cemented something that can and will never be broken. Now I look back at asking her to bring contraband into an Indian jail for me with shame.

The final visit came, and it was so sad for me to watch my mum and my son cry because of something I had done that they had no say in or bearing on. Martin, who was then 11, just stood with the tears in his eyes and my mum cried, I did too. It would be the last time I`d see them for who knows how long. They left and I watched as they left the prison, my own eyes by now filled with tears. The comedown after any visit was always pretty bad, but on that occasion it was the worst feeling I had had in my time in jail in India.

Back in the cell Mario had an idea and he would fix it for me, he proudly told me. Leave it to Mario were his exact words.

“Don’t take tension baba”, Mario will fix it for you. He then came up with the plan that I make a hospital appointment and call my mum so she and Martin could come see me there. I made the appointment and he sorted the escort out, not one rupee did it cost me.

I went to get the check for a problem I was having with my prostate gland (internal anal) and my mum, Martin, and Ashley brought some sandwiches and a bottle of 7UP for me as requested. The guards stood 50 yards away and allowed us to have a wee picnic and a nice end to their time in Goa visiting me. They left that day leaving a hospital and not some filthy and antiquated past its time Prison. We all smiled as they left, and the shitty feeling from before was not there. It was cheerio in the park, I have two Indian police escorts to thank for that. They totally refused to take one single penny from me and just made me promise if I was taking anything back to the jail I wouldn’t get caught. I promised them I was taking nothing back to the jail and I wasn’t anyhow.

I should maybe mention at this point that my mum before coming over had been asked to go round all my friends and get all their old Celtic football gear. Tops, shorts, hats, and flags arrived at Vasco Jail with my mum at the first visit. I`d say about a third of the jail were by the next evening wearing Celtic jerseys with more to come at the next visit.

Everyone was asking James Toner for a green t-shirt like all their friends had. When anyone asked for the green t-shirt they were made to sit down and listen to some of the club's history and songs, they were memory tested the next day and given their Celtic top when they passed the simple test. Not many passed the tests but they all got their tops anyway.

During the coming months in Vasco there were lads who would come and ask me if the hoops or the white International top looked ok with their jeans. They were even wearing the jerseys to court and coming back with not guilty verdicts. Even after you were found not guilty you had to return to the Jail to collect your things and for them to process you to leave, if you know what I mean.

After the second visit, there would have been about 50 Glasgow Celtic tops of varying colours and ages being paraded round Vasco Sada Jail. I of course loved it, Celtic are my team and I was spreading the word. Albeit to some pretty undesirable characters but I wasn't judging any of them. That job would be someone else`s. One of the more humorous moments in Vasco, to me anyhow, was when my friend sent me a box of duplicate Celtic tops and shorts from China. I think there were maybe twenty sets of shorts and jerseys in the box that eventually found its way to me just before Christmas 2009. The jailer, or superintendent as he was called in Vasco, asked to see me in his office. He knew me from before when he was the "big jailer" in Mapusa.

On his office desk was this unopened parcel addressed to me. He had this funny way of speaking, sort of through his nose with an added squeak to it. He eyed me with suspicion and then asked the question.

"James Toner, what is this?"

"It looks like a box with my name on it, sir."

"Go ahead and open it then."

I ripped open the box knowing fine well that it would contain some Celtic gear from China, it said so on the customs label. I took one of the packets out and opened it up in front of him. It was a hooped Celtic jersey and a pair of Celtic shorts.

"Why do you have so many of these, James Toner?" he asked with this puzzled expression on his wee face.

"Sir, you stand on your balcony every day and watch me playing football with the other prisoners. I am the only foreigner who has fully integrated into your prison and I cause you or any of your staff any problems. My friend has sent me these so I can give them to the other lads who play football with me."

"But why are you giving out so many gifts James Toner? There is something going on in my jail and I want to know what it is!" he almost squealed.

"Sir, I am sure there is plenty going on in your jail but I am involved in none of it. These jerseys are the jerseys of the football club I support in Scotland. It was the football club supported by my father and his father too. It is a tradition handed down from generation to generation, and I am not only an ambassador for my family and my country, but I am also an ambassador for Glasgow Celtic Football Club. I am merely spreading the word in your jail, sir. I have no ulterior motive and will be sure not to give these jerseys to anyone who troubles your staff, sir."

That might sound a wee bit too over the top, but words like ambassador and generation and thoughts about his staff are what these guys need to hear.

I smiled at him and said "I'm sure the jail manual doesn't say it is not allowed to give gifts or spread the word of tradition from other counties, sir."

He too smiled at that, because he was the man who had first allowed me to see the jail manual when we were both in Mapusa on opposite sides of his desk back there.

"Ok James Toner, you can take them into the jail but you cannot take them all at one time. I will allow you to take six today, six at the end of the week, and the other seven after that".

"Thank you very much sir, I appreciate you showing an understanding of our foreign culture". He knew I was taking the piss but he was laying down the terms so he had actually won in his wee mind. I think we were both ok with the outcome but he closed the deal using these words.

“James Toner, next time you get your Celtic jerseys sent, could you ask that they come in different colours?”

I had to stifle my laughter as I left his office, did a wee tiny bit of pee come out? I think it probably did.

The Celtic gear became a big thing in Vasco and my big English mate Danny used to try it on with me because he had a dislike for Celtic.

“Hey Toner, you Irish bastard, come here you stupid Fenian cunt.” He`d say to me.

“Get back to Liverpool where you belong, English wanker. We`ve got enough of you scousers in here as it is.”

He`d fume at that because he was from Manchester, but it passed some time for the both of us while causing some consternation among the jail guards who thought we were going to be having a go with one another. It was also during these wee slagging matches that we`d pass whatever contraband was being moved about. Hash, pills, or even a phone were amongst the stuff that got moved from one landing to another when Danny and I “locked horns”, and he`d throw me about, the guards didn’t want to see that so they looked away.

Whenever I dropped anything down at Danny`s cell I’d wrap it in the Celtic Newspaper or some other propaganda I had lying about. I have no doubt the guards knew, but it was easier for them to take the money I knew Danny was paying them or take the money I was paying them, albeit through a third party - Mario- and we were all happy.

Danny was my friend in Vasco, and one of the people I went to see when I knew my transfer back to Mapusa had been given the ok.

In March 2010, Danny (Ajay) Kaushal collected and saved over 30 amitriptyline anti-depressant pills and the same amount of Nitrasun Sleeping Tablets and took his own life. This hulking great bear of a man who had become my friend in such a short period of time committed suicide. He could not live with the thought of going back to the UK to do a 15-year sentence. I still cannot believe he did it.

Still before that in 2009 it was now December and the festive season was almost on us. The jail was preparing for the festivities and the prisoners were looking forward to putting on their Christmas show. For some of these guys it would be their 4th Christmas on remand for crimes most of them would be acquitted off in the end up. A fuckin Christmas show, I already hated Christmas and this was to be my first Christmas and New Year celebrations in prison.

There were some Catholic nuns who would come to all the jails once a week and try convert the unconverted or bring the stray sheep back into the fold, and the Christmas show was their idea years ago apparently. All the long term remanded took part. That word doesn`t actually exist but I used it because no one should be held for four or five years before their trial. Guilty or not guilty, again they are my own views having witnessed it first-hand.

The jail was buzzing for 2 weeks before Christmas, and before long I too was roped into the festivities. I was to speak and sing and hand out Christmas cards which the local school kids wrote for the prisoners. In the end I looked forward to the night as much as everyone else. By this time, I had no feelings about time and I had unattached myself from outside the prison and the folk I loved. This was my lot and I had learned to deal with it in the way I deal with life on the outside today, most days at least.

I could have sat and said I'm not into Christmas and been double miserable, or I could get involved and do something that would help some of these lads get past a difficult time that I had a handle on anyway. I was to introduce the proceedings and sing a Scottish song.

The day of the show all hell broke loose in the jail and I was in the middle of the shouting and bawling. We were sitting eating our lunch, so it would have been around 1 o clock, when the main sergeant came in and told us to pack, we were all being moved. He went on to tell us that there had been an emergency transfer from the central jail called Aguada and they were all being put in number 7. There were lots of empty rooms downstairs but the Aguada lads didn't fancy being underground so we were going to make way for them.

The full cell began moaning, I took it to shouting and bawling about it being dinner time and that I was going nowhere till I had eaten my dinner at least. I actually voiced that we

shouldn't be moving at all to accommodate prisoners who were serving between three and ten years, the jail manual stated that remand and convicted prisoners were not to be held together.

"Why should we be moved underground when these convicted prisoners wouldn't take being put there?" I voiced.

Folk were moaning but not really making much real noise about it. They had been told to move so they would be moving. Looking back, I don't blame them because they would have been given the bamboo massage and the normal Indian prisoner doesn't like pain. Even Mario seemed like he had resigned to the fact we had to move and made not much of a complaint at all.

Next thing I'm out on the landing shouting and telling them to go and fuck themselves, I`ll move when I've finished my lunch.

There must have been about 15 guards by this point and they were all amazed that I was not for moving.

"Go get your boss and get him to come down and tell us to our faces why we`re being moved."

I was seething that we were being treated like shite and we were all on remand, none of us had been convicted, but the Governor was moving us because the convicts didn`t like where they were being put.

Like I've said before, when I shouted they couldn't understand a word, but I used enough expletives for them to know that I wasn't happy at all and all the bloke in charge could say to me was "stop the bad language James Toner."

Mario did this running about thing he did when trying to appease everyone. He didn't want to upset any of the staff because he`d have been beaten too but he also had me, his golden calf, his golden egg-laying goose, running about looking at guards in the eye and telling them in a very broad Scottish accent that I'd bite their noses off if one of them touched me or any of my stuff.

They just thought I was a bit mad and I suppose they were right. I was trying to live somewhere between a spiritual life and surviving externally in a foreign prison. Sometimes the negative energy just spewed out of me I'm sure, other times I'd sit like the Buddha and not say one word.

The outcome was we got split up and allowed to stay above ground, but I was put into a cell with 25 people and that was about 10 too many for the size of it. One toilet that was only to be used for urinating and cleaning our plates in and if we needed the other, we had to wait till we were open between six and ten and again between two and six. Basically that's being told when you can have a shite; do any of you know how that feels?

"And you can stick your fucking Christmas show up your fuckin arse as well" being my final retort as I was moved into another crowded cell that was dirtier than the one I'd just came from and didn't afford as much sunlight through the small windows. I was raging and Mario knew it.

"Don't take tension baba, tonight we have the Christmas show and tomorrow I'll have half of these moved elsewhere".

I always felt bad about things like that, I had the money which gave me the power, and in the morning some boys were going to be moving to make our living quarters more bearable. I almost felt like I had invaded their space and put them out of it, it wasn't a nice feeling, but this was prison and I had made enough noise to get as near as to what I wanted.

I was split from the two Russians Vashya and Viktor and the Italian too. He was moved downstairs to a big cell that had 24-hour surveillance and was the most hated room in the jail. A guard sat outside the room all day and all night, and although he`d turn his back if given some paisa the Italian didn't have any money so he went underground. No windows so no sunlight. I wasn't that bothered not to be in the same cell as him any more truth be told, because he brought nothing to the party and it wasn't a charity we were running. I also didn't like the way he treated the young Indian boys who would run about after us. I always treated them well but he thought his mob were still the Roman Empire and spoke down to them and had them doing his washing, going down for his tea in the morning and anything else that needed done without being fair to them in return. Underground was good enough for him.

I suppose by mid-afternoon I had calmed down a bit and was approached by one of the lads who had put a lot into the Christmas show. I could also see he had been sent as the representative and didn't want to be the one to ask but he did.

"James, are you still going to help us with the Christmas show tonight?" My shouting and bawling had been having an effect on everyone, the prisoners as well.

I had been so selfish in my own mind thinking about my own wellbeing and comfort, these boys had worked hard to put this together, and I was to compere it and sing so I was a big part. I assured him I had calmed down and would be down there with them doing my bit when the time came.

The Christmas show's format was me introducing and thanking the superintendent for allowing us to celebrate and put on our show, the same superintendent that I had been shouting and bawling about being a wanker only hours before. After my introduction the prisoners were to perform a little comedy sketch followed by some local high school kids doing another sketch. I then sang Flower of Scotland and You`ll Never Walk Alone before the prisoners and the local kids would perform another two comedy skits.

About 150 prisoners were in the hall with various invited dignitaries, the superintendent and half the local archdiocese included.

I was given the microphone and looked around at the excited prisoners then my eye caught the superintendent's. He looked like he was expecting me to go into a rant about the afternoons carry-on, but I had no intention of spoiling it for the boys who loved just being out of their cells and in a hall all together in the run up to Christmas.

I looked at the superintendent and thanked him for allowing the evening to take place and thanked the local important people for "soiling their feet" and entering Sada Jail to watch the show. I thanked the nuns for all they did for the prisoners too.

Then the show commenced and went well with all enjoying the event. At the end of it I put on my Santa hat, which I still have, and handed out the Christmas cards to the inmates which had been written by local school kids. Then there was this procession where the Nuns gave out little Christmas bags to all the prisoners. I stood in line, and then when it came to my turn this senior nun turned round and said to me that I had been to the back of the queue and I was attempting to get 2 bags. She was adamant that I wasn't getting another one. If it hadn't been for the intervention of one of the other nuns who whispered in her ear, I wouldn't have got my bag with toothpaste and soap and a wee face cloth. The old bastard still looked at me like I was a thief and was trying to steal from them.

Thinking back now, it was quite sad that some of these lads had never had Colgate toothpaste, although I don't use it myself so I gave mine away. They all read their wee cards and put them on their walls with homemade glue. Like I have said that was made from bread incidentally, it was turned into a paste then put on the back of the cards to make them stick to the walls.

By now we had number 7 inhabited by 20 convicted inmates from Aguada who wanted to be in Vasco as much as I wanted to be in room number ten. They had the knowledge though, and the jail governor was very wary of them.

Next day he appeared on the landing and walked towards me, I was expecting shit for the way I had kicked off the day before, but he just walked up to me and said in his wee squeaky voice: "James Toner, very good performance last night. Thank you for your contribution." I had been ready for this big argument that never materialised, and so I merely thanked him for recognising the small part I had played in the event.

He had enough on his plate with these long term convicted lads who had been forced to move from their homes - they were all serving ten years for drug charges- to this shite hole that was Vasco. They were talking hunger strikes and the like, and they knew the rule book like it was Peter and Jane.

They had also used illegal mobiles to alert the press, so the full jail got spun looking for the phones they knew we had but they could never find. When they did find one it was simply a case of someone meeting a guard outside and giving him some money and a new phone. We were never without one, but my problem was that I was the only Scottish guy in the jail, and if I was talking Scottish it had to be on the phone. I was banished to the toilet to use it and the reception was often no good so I used the once a week outside call we were allowed as well.

The convicted lads were all ok and some of them had the same story as me, while others had the same story as others in the cells. They were not all innocent but not all not guilty at the same time; some of them were the victims of a politically motivated affair, and some of them just hadn't been paying the piper, and we know who calls the tune. We integrated well and I learned from these lads, some of whom had almost finished every day of a ten-year sentence. Every single day; they had served more than 3650 days with not one day off for good behaviour. Like I have said before, if they couldn't pay the bounty they had to do another year, and some of these boys were doing just that.

Just after Christmas I had caught a bad flu and it had taken its time in clearing up. One day I was lying sleeping when the gate opened and the shout of 'James Toner to a visit' went up. I wasn't expecting anyone and hadn't prepared for the visit. I trudged along the corridor looking like hell had just spat me out and I felt the same way. I walked into the visit room to one of the best surprises I had during my time in Vasco.

It was my old mate Lee who I hadn't seen for a couple of years before I left Glasgow. He was accompanied that day by big Boothy, who was Lee`s girlfriends Son. It was great to see them although he must have looked at me and at my surroundings with some concern. We chatted away and he asked if I needed anything. I asked for stamps and a piece of Charas, he told me no problem and would see me at the next visit. I would be better prepared the next time though.

The following week the visit day came round and once again I was shouted out for a visit. This time I had made sure I was shaved and my flu had been shaken off as well, so I glided along the corridor in the knowledge it was Lee back to visit me. This time he was accompanied by his misses, Shirley, and their wee lassie Ronni who was only a baby at that time. It was a nice visit because they had come out of their way on their holidays to visit, even though they were on the other side of the wall that I had built round myself that I spoke about earlier in the story. Shirley was aghast at the state of the place and asked how long I thought I'd be there; I wasn't in a position to tell her at that moment though.

I asked Lee about the Charas. He said it was in the taxi and who was he to give it to. I laughed and said he could give it to me in here. The look on his face was priceless when I said to him that it would be cool to pop back out to the taxi to get it. He would have said something like:

"Cannae fuckin dae that Jimmy."

I told him it was cool, and I wouldn't be asking if I didn't have it under control. I asked the desk sergeant if it would be ok for my friend to go out to the car to collect the bottle for the baby as he had forgotten to bring it into the jail. The old sergeant just looked and nodded for a guard to take Lee to the door and wait before allowing him back in. He came back and sat down beside me, he put the Charas on the bench and I put it into my pocket. I knew they wouldn't be searching me after the visit and knew Lee would have no problems on leaving the jail. Another great wee visit and one I'll always remember till the day I die. Again looking back at that I'm filled with shame. At that point in my life I was selfish to my core and shouldn't have asked Lee to do that. For that I'm sorry Lee.

At the end of the visit they left and I had my stamps, big bag of fresh fruit, and my lump that he had gone back out to the car to pick up. One of the first things I did when I got back to the cell was use one of the stamps to write a wee letter to Lee and Shirley thanking them for coming to see me. It would have been just as easy to enjoy their holiday in the thought that I had built my own big wall when wearing my own poor me badge, so why bother now that I was in trouble. So again I thank the three of them, if this was a text I would put a couple kisses but this is a serious book so there will be none of that.

In January I got word that another friend of mine was coming to visit me with his misses. They had actually booked to go to Spain some place but the company they had booked with went bust. He decided to use the money they got back and the time he booked off to come and visit me in India. He arranged the visits through my lawyer and got permission to come to see me twice a week, so we had four visits in the fortnight he was here.

The first visit was fantastic for us both I'm sure, although at that time I didn't know he was carrying a wee secret that was to end up more like a burden to him. He was with his misses, Irene, and they had brought me all sorts of stuff, clothes, books, and presents and letters from back home. He asked if I needed anything and I produced my shopping list of creams and shampoos and toothpastes, all expensive Ayurvedic stuff now that I was attempting to get in touch with nature and all that. Prison does that to people; Indian prison definitely did it to me.

Before he left he asked what at the time I thought was a strange question: "How much do you trust that mob along in Colva?"

I was straight back with my reply and it stands to this day.

"I trust Toff but I do not trust that wee wank Tommo."

We bade our goodbyes, and Mick and Irene left to go and enjoy the sun and their holiday. That was the plan in any case. He returned alone the following Tuesday to visit me.

Before we sat down he slipped me a right big lump of Charas and then asked how much money I thought there was in Colva. I replied that there should have been about 1300 Pounds Sterling which would have been about 100,000 rupees. Toff was holding it and had been making sure I had money in my account and bringing me fruit and whatever I needed when he came to visit me. Mick looked at me and told that he had asked for the money to put some in my account and give the biggest part to my lawyer.

He was told that this wee guy Tommo, a 55-year-old man from Blackburn, had been allowed to borrow it, but when Mick asked for it he was told that he would have to get it together. My lawyer wanted some money before my case was to start properly. Mick took it out of his own bank and paid it to him before Tommo eventually gave him 80,000 rupees. That still left a shortfall of 20,000 rupees and another 15,000 I had loaned Tommo before I had been arrested. In a letter I was to receive from Tommo in reply to one I sent him, he told me that he owed me no money. Why? Because he had helped my 70-year-old Mother out when she had missed her flight home when she came to visit. He also told me in that letter that I was where I deserved to be and that he would be back in Scotland before I was. He reckoned he`d be there by 2015, way before I got back.

Mick gave that money to my lawyer as well instead of taking it back or throwing the good things he had done in my face; a real friend I suppose you`d call him. I added that into my tale not to let people know how man can be so inhumane to man, but to thank my friend for keeping me calm and sorting out what would have been a much bigger mess if he hadn't been here to do so. Thanks very much Mick. Tommo's snide letter to me when I was in prison was ripped up that night and put in the bin. Why? I ripped it up for two reasons; one reason was that I was advised to do so by two friends who had been in prison and who knew what being in possession of such a letter could have done to my mind. The other reason was simply because to have set it on fire would have been the waste of a match, and matches were a commodity on the inside of an Indian prison. I'll be honest in saying that for a long time I had this recurring revenge fantasy of me punching wee Tommo's face to a pulp. Now I can see him for being the sick wee cunt he actually is.

Day to day life in Vasco was easy, but the one thing that still annoyed me was that it was too busy. The cells were opened at 6 in the morning till ten am, closed till two after lunch, then opened back up again till 6pm. There were always people coming and going and I couldn't get any peace. They all wanted to learn English or teach me Hindi or ask questions that only foreigners had the answers too, or so it seemed. I also became sick of the constant calling out of my name, James Toner. It ended up getting on my nerves so much that I asked for a transfer back to Mapusa.

No one could understand it, why go back to Mapusa? Locked up 22 hours every day and 23 on the Sunday because we didn't get out on a Sunday afternoon. People have this idea that in jail you have solitude, not in Vasco you didn't. Loneliness is a state of mind I once read, and now I know what that means. I could feel lonely but be surrounded by 20 yapping Indians all speaking different dialects and shouting James Toner when I walked past. That might appear trivial, but it was driving me mad. There were too many people about and I didn't like it; I had no space and got no peace.

It all came to a head one day when I was being brought back from the hospital where I was being treated for an enlarged prostate gland. The guards often hitched a lift from passing motorists rather than wait on public transport, which was how they moved you about if there weren't enough prisoners being shifted to warrant the use of an escort bus. One of the guards put his hand out and this big fucking truck stopped. In I got, followed by the 2 jail guards. We all drove back to the jail in this big dumper truck. I was livid and started writing as soon as I had got back to the busy room that was number ten in Vasco Sub Jail Sada. I wrote to the governor, I wrote to his boss, I wrote to the British Consul, and I wrote to the newspapers.

I think the thing about having a doctors finger up my arse watched by two Indian policemen, followed by being driven back to the jail in a dumper truck almost did it for me. I was taking tension and I knew it. I had to be moved or something would have had to give, and I knew I wouldn't have benefitted from anything that happened in terms of me going mad and shouting and bawling. I did it right and in quadruplicate for all the important people to read about. The news of my transfer came through in a matter of days. I'd be going back to Mapusa which I didn't particularly like, but I was getting out of Vasco.

Another thing about Vasco was its distance from the court in Mapusa; bearing in mind that my trial had been charged already, I was at fever pitch every time we went to court. Sometimes, because the bus went to Panjim before going to Mapusa and your case had been called, you were just given another date because you hadn't been in court. That was all wrong for a start. Getting up early, shaving, and getting the best clothes on and then sitting on this dilapidated bus for an hour and a half before getting to the court all set for something happening.

The bus had been late so nothing happened, and we all trooped back onto that bus with another date. This time though, because you had been charged in court and your trial had officially begun, the dates could be anything up to four or five weeks away. That is inhumane, but the British Consul thought that this was the due process and they were happy to go with it. I was told by Ms Shilpa Caldiera - in a matter of fact way and with great contempt - that "sometimes in India cases could go on for 5 years." The lady was and still is batting for the other side, and I'll go into that in more detail later too.

Before I moved from Vasco I had the pleasure of seeing Ashpak Bengre get his comeuppance too; it was very violent, but violence breeds violence and he had his coming for a long time. He had been moved from Mapusa to Vasco because he had ordered an attack on some other Goan villain who was attending court. Bengre`s goons attacked this guy with swords and axes on the steps of the High Court building. Out of the 4 assailants, one got caught and he took his bamboo massage like all Indians do, they just grass on whoever was with them when they went to do the job.

They knew Bengre was behind it and raided his cell in Mapusa, finding mobiles and sim cards which connected him to the lad who had been caught and who had informed on everyone else. So Bengre was being moved to Vasco where he had been before and had been involved in some gang shit there. He arrived one day and they put him and his co-accused into the same small cell. Next morning, he went to get his tea and 2 dry bread rolls when he was viciously attacked by a lad who he had been naughty with before. The boy helped the jail electrician and took a hammer home with him, then in the morning he hit Bengre about 4 times over the head with the hammer.

It was enough to give him about 30 stitches but without actually doing any real damage to his head.

The real attack came the following morning at the same time, only this time it was set up by the jail guards and Mario. Bengre came out for his tea, and the tea boy waited till he had turned his back and stabbed him in the side and on the head. Bengre tried to defend himself but he was also stabbed in the chest and on his arms. He didn't come back from the hospital that day, but he was photographed and pictured in the local newspapers the next day on a stretcher going to the hospital. He never came back to Vasco while I was there.

On the 12 of February 2010, I received word that I would be going back to Mapusa the following morning. That night I said my good byes to everyone, Churchill was crying but he was not the only one. I had been the first foreigner some of these lads had ever seen close up, I was definitely the first that some of them had spoken to, and I was 100% sure I was the only foreigner who had treated them as an equal. We are all human beings after all. I had written an application for a Goan guy called Suresh Redkar who came from Mapusa and he had been granted leave to go back there as well. I gave away a few wee things to some people who I had grown fond of and then prepared the leaving party.

The 12th of February that year was the Hindu Festival of Shiva Ratri. Shiva is the God who they believe gave the world Charas and Shiva smoked the stuff himself, ironic I know but I`m just telling it like it is. Hindus are allowed if not actively encouraged to smoke Charas that day in honour of the Lord Shiva, The Creator and Destroyer of the Universe. I made a big batch of milk laced with Charas and offered it round the room for everyone to take a cup. Some did with relish and we all sat stoned till they gradually fell asleep one at a time. My time in Vasco was over; I was leaving everyone behind who I had been transferred from Mapusa with. I didn't think I would miss any of them, another thing I was right about because at that time I had detached myself from my family and friends back in Scotland so leaving a bunch of rogues and rapscallions behind was no problem to me.

Chapter 14: Back to the Beach

And so it was that Saturday morning the 13th February 2010 at half past nine, I lifted my belongings and made to leave Vasco Sada Jail. I walked out on to the landing and there were forty men lined up in a sort of guard of honour, all standing waiting to say goodbye to James Toner. Was I touched by this display? Of course I was. I had been there only 3 and a half months and had made such an impression that people lined up to say goodbye to me. It was a nice moment and not one you`d anticipate in prison, a foreign prison to boot.

The return journey to Mapusa that morning was a bit different to the journey I had made 3 and a half months previously going in the other direction. I felt no fear for a start, I was going back to a jail I was familiar with, to staff I knew from before, to prisoners I knew would still be there from when I had left in October 2009. It was different this time because I knew the score now and wasn't going to be the new guy on the block. The young jailer was on duty when I got there, and they were pretty thorough in their search of me and my belongings. I wasn't giving them any of the stuff I had accumulated over the previous 8 and half months in any case, but I had no contraband.

I was allocated one of the shitty rooms at first till they could find space to put me back in number six where I had come from in the first place. Antony the Greek was in number six but he looked terrible, I was soon to find out why and although it didn't surprise me I was still a bit shocked none the less.

In my short time away he had become one of the brownies, a jail term for heroin users, like I say I was shocked but not surprised. Natasha, his girlfriend, had by this point admitted she was finished with him, and had in fact fallen pregnant to this big greasy looking Italian fuck called Andreas. I knew him from attending court because he was out on bail on a heroin charge. All`s fair in love and war they say, I don't swallow that when the guy is banged up and hasn't even had the heart or the balls to tell his mother about his arrest. It's possibly the hardest phone call you may ever make, it was for me, but it's something you have to do. I think he believed he was protecting her but come on to fuck, couldn't tell his mum. In any case, he was walking round the yard like a zombie and still looked like all he did was think. He was in effect acting and speaking like a Greek, heroin-addicted Mr Bean. Turns out he had also been getting regular slaps off some of the local prisoners in the jail, Jayesh Dhuri being one of them. He, if you recall, was the idiot who Mr Bean used to call a Mongoloid. Well that worm turned when Antony had no back up and he became the whipping boy of Jayesh the Mongoloid.

I was far from being happy in my own new cell, but I knew it was only temporary so I just got my head down and tried my best not to interact with the guys in there. Two in particular were in for sex offences and I know what I have previously stated, but to be in close quarters with one guy who had raped a nine-year-old Russian tourist, and another who buggered a 12-year-old Indian boy was not easy for me to take. I knew about the spiritual path that kept me sane, but these two gave me the boak and I told them as much.

The one who buggered the young lad said he knew my face; I told him that's right because it was me who had slapped him on his first day in Mapusa last October. I told him to keep away from me or I`d do the same and this time it would not be a slap, I said that if these guys who are your countrymen are prepared to accept your crime then I`m only a strange man in a strange land, so you have nothing to fear from me. It's not nice when you see that someone is visibly afraid of you, I know that a lot of people thrive on that shit but I don't, not then and most definitely not now.

The other younger one was as guilty as sin; he had swum out to sea where a young 9-year-old was swimming while her mother watched from the shore. He had a "friend" who had been speaking to the mother and he used that as cover to rape the little girl in the sea. They had both ran away but they were caught and the friend gave full evidence against his as yet still co-accused. I used to tell him to be ready for the two big Russians in Vasco, they are going to take turns each to fuck you and I will let them know when you are coming too.

Then when you are convicted the same will happen to you in Aguada, you will be constantly beaten and fucked for seven to ten years. He proclaimed his innocence but his story didn't stand with me and I knew it wouldn't in court.

As it turned out, they were both acquitted of the rape but the prosecution used their appeal period to attempt to bring them back from Orissa which is one of the states in the Northern part of India where these two hailed from. He hung himself before the Police could re-arrest him. Maybe out of fear of being innocent, but I didn't get that feeling and I now believe that I was starting to develop the extra senses that humans have but that have been suppressed over the years by people who don't want us to know we have them. Just a wee thought for you all to take on as you hopefully read on.

The dynamics of the jail had by now changed a fair bit, and the movement of anything illegal was down to two brothers. Their names were Rajesh and Jayesh (The Mongaloid) Dhuri. One day in the yard when I had been there a few days, Rajesh, who was in charge and the sensible one, approached me and asked if I wanted to go to his room. His reasoning was I would want a phone and they had phones, and if I was using a phone I would be less likely to tell anyone about their wee operation. Made sense to me, and he told me that in two days there would be a transfer to Vasco; we did know this was coming anyway but still didn't know who would be going. I knew one thing for sure, it wouldn't be me.

My Japanese friend Yuki Morritta was still in number six and there was a new guy who had said hello to me one day at court. His name was Olli Patric Wirkunnen, he was from Sweden and he knew Henke and Celtic so we hit it off straight away. They were both in six with the brothers and Antony. It wasn`t till after the transfer that I finally found out how mad Antony had got and how close to the edge Yuki was at this time as well.

The transfer came and I was moved to number 6, Antony was sent to Vasco. I feared for him in that jungle because he could hardly bear to be in the small Mapusa cage never mind in the jungle with lions and the tigers and circling sharks in case you made it to the sea. I`m not a writer so I can hope you all see I'm writing in metaphors here, its magick being able to write what you want because it's my story. I can't recall but I hope I started it with once upon a time.

I`ll start off by telling you about the Dhuri Brothers; one had been caught with a kilo of Charas, he had called his brother and friend and they in turn called the village councillor. He turned up and the four of them were arrested on possession of one kilo, the C.B.I was also involved so they had two cases to answer. The CBI is the Indian F.B.I. A right shitty mess but they were making the most of it, and although not big or nasty they did run the jail from their position in number six, Rajesh at least. The younger Brother would incur my wrath before I left Mapusa, which would be sooner than I thought it would be as it transpired.

Then there was Yuki who by now also looked pretty bad, and that was down to tension, a tension caused by that fuckin arab David Abraham stealing his lawyer's money to pay for his own lawyer, the same lawyer incidentally as my own, and by the time I had left Vasco he had also "borrowed" 20,000 rupees from me as well. I thought I was helping the guy out to get him out of jail. That's what people in jail do for other people in jail if they are in a position to do so. I would meet him again on the other side of the wall and for the believers in karma, I`m not one anymore, he got what was coming to him and then some.

Then there was the Swedish lad Olli who I bonded with straight away, we both enjoyed our Charas and a wee selection of pills and we both kept ourselves to ourselves. It pretty soon became me and Olli against the rest in that room, not quite everyone, but we took no shite from any of the brothers who at the end perhaps wished they hadn't invited me into their wee castle.

They were both Hindus, as were all the guards. They had a couple of guards under their wing or in their pocket, so the cell had everything but they were not operating a charity, in fact far from it as it happens. They were charging 100 rupees for a 2-rupee bag of carcinogenic tobacco. This stuff was not for smoking, it was to be chewed but people smoked it and it stank the place out. Olli used to burn it on tinfoil before putting it in his joints; the black acrid smoke that came off it should have been enough to put anyone off. I, as you may recall, have this perverse sense of pride that I have never smoked a joint in my life. Pipes, bongs, buckets, and hot knives yes, but that tobacco fuckin kills you man, says so on the packet for fuck sake.

The brothers also had the phone system in operation, and I had to hand it to them for their ingenuity in that respect. The younger one - who was fuckin stupid - came over to me and asked if I wanted to buy a phone, a cheap bottom of the range Nokia that would have cost about 1000 rupees outside. He asked for 10,000 rupees, but threw in a couple of incentives that made a blatant attempt at extortion seem like a right good deal. As it turned out it was a good deal as well. He took the phone off me in the morning and hid it during the day, he then gave me it back after lockdown fully charged. I got someone to meet a friend of his and give him the money for the phone, a hassle free deal, and one which worked right up until I left Mapusa again. There was now me, Olli, and Yuki in with 5 Goans, and the constant noise was worse than before. They didn't or couldn't read, they played noisy card games and an even fuckin noisier game called Karam. Played on a flat board with pool type pockets and using thick poker chips as the balls, it involved aiming and pocketing the chips. 'Click-clack' was followed by raucous laughter and often arguments. 75% of Goan people are proper cunts, there, I said it. They are also afraid when someone speaks back to them, and that is what eventually happened in their room.

Like I said, me and Olli had kept ourselves to ourselves, it's the way to go in jail, getting the head down it would be known as in Scotland. But I made a big mistake in Mapusa that second time around and it took me a while to get back from it. I tried to get sleeping pills off the weekly doctor but she referred me to the clinical psychiatrist; he asked me about my situation and my past life and if I had any history of mental illness, no smiling please.

I told him about my brother and about the false case and the noise in Mapusa, I just wanted the sleeping pills and I'd be out of there. He said I was clearly depressed and he would be recommending some inpatient treatment for me; no chance doctor, I told him. I just couldn't sleep, just give me something to slow my mind down at night. He was having none of it, so before I knew it I was being prescribed Prozac, Xanax and Lorazepam. The happy pill, the nerve pill, and the sleeping pill were what I left that hospital with that day, and it was one of those regimes where you didn't self-medicate; you were given your tablets and were watched while you were taking them.

So I was now happy, my nerves were calm, and I slept, but continued usage of these drugs fucks you up even more than how fucked up you might have been in the first place. Olli liked the Xanax and I liked the Lorazepam. We just swapped them about and his nerves were calm and I slept like a wee happy baby.

By this point Yuki had developed three personalities, four even. He was Yuki who would dress down into small pants and rolled up t-shirt to make like a bra top. He had thick long black hair and he`d put that in ponytails and become Yuki's 'sister'. He would stand at the gate and shout on the guards then sing Nirvana`s 'Rape Me' when they came to see him. The guards didn't know what to do with him, but he went from bad to worse. One day he sat beside me and told me about the Arab and how he had stolen his money and that he was afraid of going to Aguada for ten years. None of us wanted that to happen, and we knew that if he could find the money the lawyer would win his case. He told me it was fine and that he had called his grandfather who was going to send him the money to pay the remainder of the lawyers' fees. Then he came out with this crazy question which on reflection was maybe intended to shock me, I`m still not sure.

I should point out that Yuki was, still is, and always will be my friend. My heart bleeds now when I think what was to eventually happen to him.

"James, do you rike brow job?" He asked.

“Yes Yuki, blow jobs are fantastic man.”

“You have made brow job?’ He enthused.

“I have had my fair share of good blow jobs, Yuki.” I smiled at him.

“No, have you ever made brow job. Have you ever given a brow job?”

I told him I hadn’t and it wasn’t really my thing, I much preferred the ladies performing their part and I would play mine accordingly. I asked him if he had, and he told me yes, he had twice, once when 16 for a dare in Japan, and another time for 1 gram of methamphetamine off some Arab fella, also in Japan.

I didn’t at the time, but I am now thinking about the differences in Japan youth culture and the youth culture I was socialised in. We were making outrageous jumps out of windows and across gaps at the top of 20 story high blocks of flats, while Yuki was giving his mates brow jobs. I now realise that Yuki was not your normal Japanese guy though. He left the structure that his parents instilled behind and was into Nirvana, drugs, and anything else that was shock horror culture.

“I make you brow job James, I have very good technique.”

I of course declined, none of you can say any different, and told him to stop all the brow job talk.

His other persona was a little more disturbing for me and Olli and for the guards. It was Nanga Baba which literally translated means 'naked baby.' He would strip off all his clothes and walk about the cell naked, go to the cell gate, and freak the guards out. They would threaten him, but he was sick and they didn't beat him. They were making plans to have him shipped though, that was for sure. The main problem about the Nanga Baba was he only did it when prompted by the Brothers Dhuri; Yuki had nothing except anything we gave him so they took advantage of it. They got him to massage their legs and arms in exchange for one of these wee pouches of 2-rupee tobacco. He did what they asked him and I hated to watch it.

They would shout Nanga Baba and he would strip and go to the gate and start banging it for attention. I told him to get his clothes on and to stop letting them two make a fool of him. He was past telling though, and it was a sorry thing to watch almost daily.

"Yuki stop taking your clothes off when these fucking little wanks say so, they are making a fool of you and driving you mad."

"What's wrong James, are you shy?" He just didn't get it and I eventually stopped trying. I knew he would be getting shipped and if he was lucky it would be to another jail, if not it would be the mental hospital. I know that isn't what we call them nowadays, but in India that is what they are, mental hospitals.

It all came to head one night when they had tobacco and he wouldn't take his clothes off for the Nanga Baba show. I could see him fuming and knew what was going to come. No Bruce Lee or Jackie Chan, he just attacked them both in a flurry of punches and kicks. They shit themselves and I managed to get in between Yuki and them, but by now it was too late. Their shouts had alerted the guards and Yuki was dragged out of the room and put into another cell. He would be moved in the morning now for sure.

And in the morning he was moved, luckily enough for him to Vasco and not to the mental hospital his behaviour actually merited at that time. The brothers were in shock and the laughing stock of the place, behind their backs for many, though they still did control most of what came into the jail and where it went to. We had an extra space now and wondered who to bring to the room. The choice was taken out of our hands about two days later.

Olli was at court when the gate opened and in walked this big hulk of a man, he looked round and put his stuff in Olli's place. I looked at the two brothers because this was not normal protocol; they quickly averted their gaze and left it to me to see if I would say anything.

I introduced myself and told him that he was on another man's spot and his own place was at the door or the gate. Last in gets the worst spot I explained to him. He just looked at me and I told the brothers to tell him in the local language what I just said, he was by now lying down on Olli's bed.

They spoke to him in the guttural high speed language that Konkani is and he looked at me in disgust. To be fair, he picked up his gear and moved towards the door but I didn't want a 6 foot 2 ape that went by the name of "Tarzan" as my enemy and I was pretty annoyed with the brothers and told them so. If it had been some wee out of state guy he would have been made to sit and face the interview panel, take a couple of slaps or punches and kicks depending on his alleged offence. He just sat and stared right through me at all times.

Olli and I would sit in his wee corner which had a blind spot and he`d light my pipe with matches and we`d get stoned. No one else took the Charas, so that suited us well, Tarzan would just sit and stare.

After two nights of this, I said to Olli I think Tarzan wants in to our two-man gang; he asked what I meant and I told him to watch. He lit my pipe and I took a big puff from it and turned to Tarzan.

"Tarzan, do you smoke Charas Baba?"

His eyes lit up and he came over to Olli's wee corner. which was always a right mess incidentally. Tarzan smoked the pipe and went and lay down, he enjoyed his puff and fell asleep like a big baby. Tarzan was now on our side and the brothers knew it, the guy liked to smoke Charas and they didn't, doesn't take a rocket scientist to work out which corner he`s going to stand in after that. I only had one small fall out with them, and again it happened when Olli was out of the room on another appointment some place.

I have already described dinner or lunch time in Mapusa, and this lunch time Olli wasn't there. The procedure was his mate would collect his lunch for him and take it back to the cell, cover the plate with newspaper and he`d get it when he came back. That's what happened that lunch time and I sat the dinner at Olli`s place in the room.

As I sat down the younger of the two brothers walked over and lifted the paper off Olli`s plate.

"What are you doing Jayesh?" I asked him.

"None of your business, it's not your plate." He snapped back at me.

"Well I'm making it my business because it's definitely not your plate and Olli is my friend, so leave it alone and eat your own dinner."

We ate sitting in a circle with our plates at our feet between crossed legs, eating with the right hand of course. This idiot couldn't let it go though.

"You think this is your room but it's not, you're not the boss in here." He said in a tone that if I had closed my eyes could have come from a seven-year-old kid.

"Jayesh, we have no boss in here but I can assure you of one thing; if we did it most definitely would not be you. Now shut your mouth, people are trying to eat their dinner here."

Under his breath he called me a fucking bastard.

I told him that when the dinner was finished I would show him who the fucking bastard was and was surprised by his reaction. He jumped up and so did I, but people got between us and I told him again to wait till people had eaten and we would speak about it. He knew what I meant by that.

His older brother suggested I leave the room and go to another one, I told him to think again and if his brother couldn't speak to me in the proper manner it would be him that would be leaving the room. I reminded him we were all adults and that we should attempt to speak about our differences, they didn't want me to move because I knew all their secret hiding places and they didn't know who would be coming in at my back. Dinner passed and plates and cups were washed and the normal thing was for some fruit to be handed out by whoever's turn it was. Today Jayesh would be giving his bananas out, be interesting to see how the little kid that he was handled this tough assignment.

He walked round the room with his bananas handing them out then came to me and looked at me and took one off the bunch.

“James Baba, do you want one of my bananas?”

“Thanks very much Jayesh.” I said as I took the piece of fruit off him. I think he would have been relieved at that outcome, but I know his brother definitely was because he was the brains and Jayesh the stupid idiot of a younger brother. All the while Tarzan had stood in the wings waiting on the nod, I`m sure they were more than aware of that as well.

Again I wrote and read and smoked with Olli and Tarzan, he would be getting bail soon enough because his case was only attempted murder, yes only, or a half-murder as it is known as in the Indian Justice system. He enjoyed joking with me and Olli, and spoke with us more than he did with his local cell mates. He loved pulling faces behind Jayesh and Rajesh`s backs and threatening to beat them, we laughed but told him to leave it out.

Another indication that I was getting better or the medication was working was when we spoke about my case. He was a taxi driver who knew Omkar Mahalaxsmi very well. He would chop him when he got out, for James Baba he would have done anything. I did think about it, but thought that if I was letting more serious things go then I couldn’t pick and choose what I didn’t let go. My attitude at that time was fuck him, he will get what's coming to him, and when it does it will have nothing to do with me. Tarzan said anytime, but I was adamant that I had left that part of this experience behind me; I still feel the same way today.

It must by now have been the end of February, and things began to stir in the underbelly of the paradise that is Goa. It all began when a girlfriend of an alleged Israeli drug dealer secretly filmed him in meetings and talking about his connection with the ANC and how he could do this and that. There were mentions of high ranking police officers, as well as the Home Minister at the times son. Well they say hell hath no fury like a woman scorned. This lady went on to reap her revenge in a very public manner indeed.

Her name is Lucky Farmhouse and she was a Swedish model, his name is Atala, an alleged Israeli drug dealer. She uploaded all her surveillance on to the very public forum of YouTube, they were taken off. She put them back on again and this time they showed Atala speaking of PSI Ashish Shirodkar and of his connection with the ANC. He spoke of how they supplied him his drugs and how he could do whatever he pleased because he had the protection of Ashish and his boss, the politician's son. The politician was named as Ravi Naik and his son was Roy. I am not making any of these allegations. They have been well documented in the local press, on the internet, and even in the Goan Parliament where the opposition leader at the time demanded the arrest of the son.

At the end of March, the first arrests were made. PSI Ashish Shirodkar was arrested along with four other ANC officers, two of whom were present on the day of my arrest. The full jail was buzzing because these were the guys who had arrested most of the drug cases in the jail. It was difficult to contain the excitement because I knew that PSI Punaji Gawas - the man who had arrested me – would soon be arrested too. I thought at that point that things had taken a turn for the better, and it would not be long before they would have to throw all our cases out. Their evidence would now be tainted for sure, well yes, but this is India and Indians are in no hurry to do anything but fleece you. Nothing racist in that statement, it's based on empirical research done by me over the past 20 years and proven beyond doubt in the past 40 months.

This is what had been happening and although I suspected it all along, I didn't know how deep it ran. The ANC had been arresting people on drug charges for the past ten years and instead of destroying any of the confiscated drugs, they simply put them back on the market again. They were, allegedly, giving them to the Israelis and to the local Goan boys to sell, and occasionally they would plant some of it on a foreigner who had been daft enough to allow himself to be lured in to buy smaller pieces in the first place. If any of this sounds familiar, it's because it should. I had gone to buy Charas from Omkar Mahalaxsmi, the amount I bought belonged to the Police. Is this starting to make sense to you now, all you people who are still thinking there isn't something right about all this? Well read on please, because it wouldn't be long before it all became like a big complicated jigsaw falling into place. But by then there had been some dramatic developments in my own trial.

On the 17th of March, my trial had begun in earnest and the first witness was the doctor who tested the drug to see that it was indeed Charas. He came and gave his evidence that I won't go into in any detail at this moment, but the following day my advocate sent word to Scotland that if my friends sent 1500 pounds he would apply for bail for me. I told him to hold off because I had always been told that bail would never be granted in my case. I called the office and Raju came to see me. I asked him what it was all about, and reminded him of his own words about bail being out of the question.

"Has Peter ever told you bail would be out of the question James?" He asked.

"No he hasn't, Raju."

"Then perhaps you should get your friends to send the money James, Peter wouldn't be applying if he didn't think he could win you bail."

I went back to my cell and thought about the conversation with Raju. After lock up I called or text Scotland and told Tosh that I thought they could get me it. He said he would get the money together for the application, he spoke to some other people and they chipped in for the bail application. At this moment I don't really know who all put money in for that, but I do know that Edward, Peter, Mooney, Asa, Big John and Tam, Tosh, Porky, and I don't know who else did. I know that whoever has sent me money or contributed to my bail application didn't do it so they could get a mention in some story that might never even see the light of day, but I thank them all from the bottom of my heart. Raju came and I signed the application and then had to listen to the jail lawyers telling me that bail wasn't possible and to forget about it. Peter had fleeced you out of 100,000 rupees. My argument to that was he could have done that at any time during the past 11 months so why do it now? I could feel a sort of desperation among some of them that it could be possible that I might be getting bail. I suppose jail does that to some folk, others were just as excited as I was myself.

For three weeks I heard nothing more about it, but a couple of the guys in the jail thought that Peter might have something, he was applying on the basis of the evidence given by the doctor who examined the Charas as I said, and he would be arguing that they couldn't say how much of the stuff was actually the drug and how much was the other adulterated crap that it was mixed with. It had been used before, but not in a long time so I held out hope.

During the time between me signing and me going back to court on the 23rd April, Tosh and his wife Janie had come back out to visit me in jail, and of course to enjoy the last of the season time before the monsoon came back round again. He came to visit me and wee Janie was a bit struck by the conditions that I was kept in; just as well neither of them had seen Vasco Sada.

The morning of the 23rd of April came, and I got set to go to court hoping the next witness would be there at least. I got to the court and there was Tosh and Janie, I'm sure she would have had her camera with her because she always did and was always snapping away with it. The court was empty that morning which was always a pretty ominous sign that nothing was going to happen that day as regards court proceedings. Then the judge came out of her chambers, and we all stood up and she sat down and we followed suit. No lawyer or anyone was in the court to prosecute or represent me either.

"James Toner." The clerk called out my name. I stood up and walked to the dock and sat down. The judge looked at me and then to a piece of paper she had in her hand.

"James Toner, you are hereby granted bail on the condition of one local surety of one lak rupees, and under the condition that you cannot leave the state of Goa and that you report to the office of the ANC every Monday morning."

I turned to Tosh and mouthed that I had been granted bail, but the judge stood up and left the court and then I was quickly taken away by the guards back to Mapusa. That weekend was to be the longest weekend of my life and I have had some long weekends in my time. I walked back into the jail and the young jailer looked at me.

“They have granted me bail, sir.”

“I am very happy for you James Toner.” He said and I`m sure he meant it. He would also have been pretty pleased to get me out of his jail, I`m equally sure of that.

I walked back to the cell and could not contain my joy at the judge’s decision. I ran in and told Olli but in front of everyone else as well. He was delighted for me as was everyone else in my room, at the afternoon exercise I`d tell everyone else, but I`m sure that anyone in earshot would have known that I had been granted leave to get to fuck out of that little hole I had begun to call home.

Olli and I formulated a plan that when the medicine came round later we would be doing a terrible thing, and we would be stealing as much of anyone else’s that we could. Like I said the long weekend lay before me, and I knew it would be early Monday evening before I was allowed out when the formalities were taken care of. I text Tosh and he was over the moon and had spoken to Peter; they had to go with the local person on the Monday morning to Peter's office and things could be taken care of from there.

In the yard that afternoon all the people I spoke to were the ones who I knew that would be genuinely happy that I was the one getting out, and not any of the false bastards who wished it was them but would never have said so to your face. Then night-time came around, and the old guard who gave out the meds came to our cell gate and handed over the bag to Olli who he trusted. Olli dropped it behind the TV and out of his sight, and we both picked out some extra sleeping pills for me and Xanax for him. We had our weekend supplies and we also had a lump of Charas, so we did what we always did; we took a couple of sleeping tablets and got stoned and drifted away into one of them hot sleeps that only medicine can bring you. I would have been dreaming that night I`m sure, but I can't say I remember any of them specifically.

The Saturday came and it was just like any other week day, people came and went to court or to the doctors or dentist so it passed pretty quickly, but the Sunday was always the long day in the jail because you only got one outside break. But to be honest it all passed in a stupor for me. I was doped up that full weekend, and I could only think of getting out and what I was going to do when I did get out on the Monday.

Monday morning came and I had a message on my phone from Tosh, there was a wee problem. We had understood that there was only one local surety required and one lak, but when he went to Peter's office on the Monday morning he was told it was two locals and two laks. He then had two problems; one was the obvious lack of another Goan to put the other 100,000 rupees into their bank account, and the other was the fact that he had only 70,000 rupees left with him. He was due to fly home on the Tuesday, and had planned to leave me with the 70,000 he had till we got something sorted about how I was going to live for the 6 months or the year I`d be on bail.

He travelled the 60 kilometres back down to Colva and headed for the shack he would have been spending most of his time at on the beach. It was owned by a local guy called Patrick who just happened to have a Scottish wife called Sandra. He explained the dilemma to Sandra and she went into the back and told her husband; without even being asked he offered to go the other local surety and he also loaned Tosh the other 30,000 rupees he was short of to cover the bail. Patrick left his shack and headed with Tosh, Janie, and Joaquin the taxi driver who was going to provide the other bond. I don't know for sure, but can only imagine Tosh's head would have been buzzing heading back up there hoping to be in time to catch the court before it closed. Missing it would have meant another night inside for me, and that might not sound like all that much considering I had been there almost one year, but when you think you're getting out and don't its sore. I had watched people getting all set for the past 11 months now and saw them being let down.

He wouldn't have been letting me down personally, but in his head he would have been. As it happens, he reached the court on time to complete the deal and text me to tell me he was coming to get me. He then texted to say he was at the gate and it would be another twenty minutes before they would let him in to get me out of Mapusa Judicial Lock Up, fancy name for a wee shite place.

I had all the things I was taking with me ready and in bags to be shifted when Mungledas came round with the evening dinner. What side they starting feeding first would determine when you got your gate opened then closed again for the night. That night they started opening number one first and made their way round to number six eventually.

"Khana Kaya." Said the guard, indicating dinner time.

I smiled when I told him I wasn't hungry and didn't want dinner that night; he looked at me and smiled back.

"Then bring your bags, James Toner, your bail has come."

I stood up and shook everyone's hand in the room then gave Olli a big hug, part of me was afraid for him being left there and not knowing if or even when he would be allowed out himself. Olli had also been part of a police set up; he had been caught with some Charas, but they tried to get money from him by producing two bottles of liquid and claiming they contained LSD. That meant that Olli would be in custody for at least a year before his report would come back. As it happened he was in for a bit longer, but in the end his report came back as being negative for LSD and he was too granted bail. They stole 15 months of that guy's life too.

The guard was now trying to hurry me up, but I wanted to go to another couple of cells to say goodbye to folk. DD was still in Mapusa, he was the guy who stood up on my first day and told me that everyone knew my story and showed me my wee wet spot on the floor, made sure I got to sleep under the fan, and in general showed this stranger some kindness. He knew I was getting bail and was genuinely over the moon for me. I told him all would be well and he would be home to his wife and children soon enough, and we could meet again. He was acquitted not long afterwards and I did get to meet him again on more than one occasion. Like before when I left Vasco, everyone wanted to say goodbye but the guard was having none of it. Not out of badness but for security reasons; he had to get me to the office, count all the heads, and make secure all the gates. I waved and walked along the same corridor I had first walked when I arrived, only this time in the opposite direction towards the small office. The young jailer sat there with my paperwork in front of him, he looked happy for me or was it for himself? He looked happy none the less anyway.

I could see Tosh and Janie outside with Joaquin the taxi driver and a stranger I had never seen before. They looked pretty excited to see me, and I was glad to be going out that gate to touch them. The young jailer once again shook my hand and wished me all the best, and added that what went before should be forgotten about. I wondered what had gone before.

They opened the gate and I shook the guards by the hand, they always treated me properly and with total respect, not only here in Mapusa but in Vasco Sada jail too. No brutality, no discrimination, just guys doing a shite job for a shite pay and not looking for any other shite to make things worse.

I stepped outside and threw my arms around Tosh while Janie took her pictures of the event. I still have my leaving jail picture sitting where I can see it. I was introduced to the stranger with the thick black beard; his name was Patrick, and it was he who had gone the other surety for me and loaned Tosh the money to make up the bail total. He had this mad look about him that in the months coming I would get to know was because he actually was mad, in a nice sort of way though. I was standing outside that jail with Tosh, Janie, and two of the very few Goans I could or ever would trust again in my life. It was a fantastic feeling to be out of prison; I had been let out of prison before, but this time it felt so much different and that is because it was totally different.

Epilogue

I thought I was fine when I left that place, and when I was writing that section of this story I did so from my memory of it as I remember it to be today. Time alters the way we perceive events though, and I was actually sick when I left that prison although I would have argued with anyone who might have said so. It's only now that the middle section is almost complete that I have actually looked at my jail diary which I kept from January till April 2010. Something deep inside me drove me through that time, and the time before that too I suppose, but it wasn't that I was this strong character or any of that shit. The diary never lies if you are honest when you are writing it, and I was honest in the things I wrote about as they actually happened and not from a memory of sections through time.

The Jail part of my story is over, but I think it only fair to share with you some of my thoughts and feelings from the time as they were occurring, it is little wonder the psychiatrist diagnosed depression and put me on happy pills, nerve pills, and sleeping pills.

Jail Diary

Friday 1st January 2010

Today sees the beginning of 2010 and I am still incarcerated in Vasco Sada Jail; it has been over 7 months since my arrest. The past week with Christmas and New Year have seen a slump in my morale which wasn't helped by a nasty flu I picked up on Boxing Day, but the time of the year played no small part in my mood. I am not a fan of Christmas or indeed the New Year, but when you are so far away from your family it is hard to block it out.

The past weeks has seen a couple of serious incidents involving Bengre. He was first attacked with a hammer one day, then the following he was stabbed quite severely. He is a murderer and extortionist, not that I`m saying that in itself is bad. I`m not going to be the one who judges him just as he won`t be the one who judges me. I do cringe though when I think that I built a sort of friendship with this guy when I was first arrested in May, a bastard who takes money from poor coconut sellers and calls it organised crime.

My own situation here is at a standstill; my case still hasn't been charged in court which means it hasn't actually begun officially as yet. It is becoming more and more difficult for me to keep things in the here and now. I cannot help being frustrated by the lack of movement in the trial.

I am also having second thoughts about my legal team and their ability to get me out of here at the end of the trial. I have had my charge sheet for almost 2 months, but still no one has come to look over it with me and explain what my chances are, good or bad. They don't come cheap, and I will be looking for some sort of guarantee before I hand over the rest of the legal fees due to them. I don't want to be left here forever and I feel that I am just a wee pawn in their big game. I am back at court on the 4th of January when I will hopefully know a bit more about the situation.

January 4th

Its India man, and that's what I have to continually remind myself. I left Vasco Jail at 1.30 to go to court and the jailer told me that I would be going by public transport. That meant me and my two escorts getting one bus to Vasco Town, another to Panjim, and then a third to Mapusa for my 2.30 appearance. We arrived at 3.15 just in time to see my lawyer cross examining a policewoman in another case, that of the Arab David. Peter destroyed the lady, she ended up crying and having to leave the stand. Some people are not cut out to be telling lies; she was one of those people.

The result for me is that my case still hasn't been charged or started properly. Peter and I ended up having words outside the court, the result of which is I have even less confidence in them now than before. He is the best in Goa though, so I have to be even more patient and do have to trust him completely or I`m fucked. The plan is to get more writing done and start to get fit, we`ll see though.

I got back to the Jail at 6 in the evening; it is like a mix of Hogan's Heroes and Dad's Army, if you can imagine such a thing. My cell is fucking roasting because one of the fans is broken, the one above my space on the floor. I have complained about it but we shall see what happens when the morning comes. My writing isn't quite in the style of a Shantaram, but it is all true and is my personal experience and is written in a Glasgow sty-lee.

Friday 8th

My application for a transfer back to Mapusa must be about near to being granted. All of the NDPS cases here want to move back; the jail is only 5 minutes from the court and although the facility is smaller, there is no Goan jail politics to contend with (stabbings and hammer attacks like). I`m handling my time in jail ok but would be a liar if I was to say I wasn't missing my family and some of my friends back in Glasgow. I would also be telling lies if I said I wasn't missing some female company, a wee cuddle or a nice kiss. That said there are more than a few blokes in here who wouldn't mind how thick or bushy your moustache was.

Wednesday 18th

There was a bit of turmoil in the jail today caused by the lads from Aguada; they are convicts who are serving from ten to thirteen years so they know their rights. Apparently each prisoner is to be fed with 100grams of fish per day, but one of the Aguada lads questioned the weight in his portion. This resulted in plates being thrown about and bedlam on my landing. This brought the superintendent down to see what the problem was. In the middle of the mayhem one of my next cell neighbours said to me that the "super" had lost control of the jail. I agreed, but he laughed and said no James, look.

One of the jail's "mental" patients was rolling about the floor with a small bandage tied to his ankle and clutching it like he had been shot. Pure theatre this was, and I asked how much the ticket for the show cost? My humour though was sometimes lost in translation and he asked what I meant. Every day brings a new picture, and each one has its own hero playing the lead role, sometimes I am even the hero myself. I didn't realise it at the time, but there were about seventy-five different movies going on in Vasco during my time there. My own being the only one I really cared about or played a proper part in.

Just back from the shower block, try the old jungle toilets at Celtic Park, mixed with Glastonbury's actual flowing river of piss, and add a touch of the toilets in Trainspotting, and there you have a wee picture of it. Having to shower or shave or brush your teeth in among that lot is not nice or healthy either I don't think. *If it wisnae fur yer wellies where wid ye be*. Knee deep in other cunts piss and groggers is the answer to that. I need to get out of here and not the way it actually felt while I was living it. I can now look back at it if not with a sort of fondness, but certainly a memory that has been clouded by time and Prozac, Xanax, and Lorazepam. I was told when I left the Jail to stay on the medication till my trial was over. I firmly believe if I had done so I would not be sitting here typing about my experience today. To put it bluntly, I would be dead, I would have killed myself either with intent or accidentally, but I would no doubt be dead.

What about the people I left behind in Mapusa and Vasco that I formed an attachment with? I would only call two of them my friends, but I did become sort of attached through the circumstances we found ourselves in with more than those two.

Anan Kumble: He was the Indian who met us at Vasco on my first night there; he was found guilty of murdering the British lady and given life in jail. Four weeks into his sentence he hung himself from the bars of the toilet window; guess his conscience couldn't bear the thought of living the rest of his life in jail.

Mario Fernandez: Mario was the top boy in Vasco when I was there, another lady killer. He was found not guilty and is now somewhere in Goa living his life again, but he did kill his ex-girlfriend. I know that because he told me. It appeared everywhere I went on my release, I bumped into this man who exuded negative energy but with this evil look added to it. I met him in Palolem two years on the trot and told him lies about my room and who I was sharing with. I didn't want anyone like him in my life and he could smell an opportunity to leach off me again. Remember he has committed the most heinous act a man can on another; he had killed, and what would have been stopping him killing and robbing me too. Then I moved up north near the end of my trial and I met him again a few times, and again he wanted to know who, where, and what type things. An evil individual if there ever was one I met here.

The Arab and the Italian: They both took a deal where they pled guilty and were released. They called it a 'convict and release'. I don't know where the Italian is and I wish him well wherever he may be. The Arab thought he was too cool for school and began working for the police who had arrested me, the ANC, but in the jurisdiction of another force. He was set up to fall and is now back in jail facing charges, which if he is found guilty will get him 15 years. Never thought I`d hear myself saying this, but not a day too long for that dirty conniving rat bag. I hope he rots in hell because he was playing the double agent and people fell because of him.

Yuki Morritta: My friend from Japan, the most altruistic person I met during my time in jail here. He had been fucked by the Arab for money, and when I had last seen him he was on the verge of insanity. He was eventually acquitted of all charges too, but his story doesn't end there. He was released in July 2010, but in the November the same year he was arrested going into Bali with a suitcase containing six kilograms of Charas. In April 2011, he was sentenced to 18 years in prison for his smuggling offence in a country that carries the death penalty for trafficking drugs through it. What had happened in his head that made him do that? He came from a country that has a very civilised order of social structure, but he had decided to live outside that and live in India. I think about Yuki all the time, a sad waste of a young life if ever there was one. *Note: Yuki Morritta hung himself in jail in Bali in 2016. I discovered that doing an internet search. A good cunt who was always going to die before his time.*

The Two Russians: Both were granted bail but Viktor ran away. He got to the Nepalese border, dropped his backpack, and made for the woods. He made it out of Nepal and is currently in South Asia some place living on a houseboat. You have to take your hat off to him, but he is currently on an Interpol wanted list and will be brought back if he is ever caught. He could well be convicted and given ten years if they do catch up with him. Vashya the other Russian got bail too; he wrote a book and got 500 copies of it published here in Goa. It's in Russian so his market is small, but he gets by and is still awaiting his trial.

The last I spoke to him he had just finished turning it into an audio book for the lazy Russians who don't want to read, nothing about it being for blind folk. Just Russians are a weird lot. That's not racist; it's again based on empirical research and the fact that Vashya - who I now call my friend - has told me the same thing himself.

Antony the Greek: He too got bail and potters about here and there doing this and that. Mr Bean turned out to be a proper selfish rat. He had been fortunate enough to have kept his passport and used it to leave the country via Nepal and head back to Greece. There he simply got a new passport and returned to India by the way he had left. He travels from India to Nepal to renew his visa, and I`m sure spin his poor old mother whatever line of Greek bullshit he always spoke. The Greek has a guest house in Goa and one in the mountains, and you aren't in a position to do that unless you are working with the police or other Goan informers. We had words when he thought I was putting too much about Goa on my Facebook and haven't spoken since. He turned bad, and will be one of the ones putting the foreigners in to the police in years to come. Malaakas. (Sub Note) Antony too is no longer with us. Mr Bean got cancer and died in 2013. Sad.

Olli: Olli my friend, who I went to visit on countless occasions and broke all sorts of rules to do so. He got bail and is still cutting about Goa playing poker and making money from the Indians who think they can play poker. I sent him a text a couple of weeks ago saying I was going to come and visit him when it suited him. He told me he was busy with the poker and when I was in the area I should call him. I texted him back and reminded him he lived 70 kilometres away, and if I was in the area it would be to see him. He didn't reply and I haven't called, make of that what you will. I have seen Olli a few times since writing and he seems more reserved than he did in jail. He stays way north of me. Olli will always be my friend.

And then there is me. I thought that the hard part was over and it would be another eight or ten months before my case was finished. I believed that I would be allowed back to Scotland to be with my son and my mother. That was not to be the case unfortunately, but it may well have been a blessing in disguise. I don't think I was ready to go back straight away. I believe that I was meant to be here that bit longer to learn about a few 'things'; I use the word 'things' to mean me, other people, and life in general, although I do intend to try and explain what 'things' have helped me through this experience which a couple of years previously would have been the death of me.

I believe the most important thing I have done in the past 28 months and at the time of writing is CHANGE. I had changed before but fell back the way, turned back into the darkness, but this time I have changed and am heading towards the light with no intent on ever turning back again. If that sentence conjures up a vision of pillars of salt then good, my writing is getting better. If the sentence doesn't bring that vision into your mind's eye, then that's good as well because it was never the intention to do so.

I remember when I was 1-year free from drinking alcohol and had my first AA birthday; some old timer wished me well and said that the hard work started there. I thought to myself, old cunt, how dare he try to rain on my parade. It wasn't long before I understood what he meant though. I mention that because it is akin to me thinking that the hard part of my shift was over because I had been allowed out of prison after 11 months on bail. I was soon to realise that was not the case as well. The hard part of the 'thing', the experience, the "section through time" was about to begin. The term "sections through time" I first heard used by Grant Morrison when he described the human beings' life on earth. Being pointed in the direction of Grant Morrison, I've got Alan McGee to thank for that, helped me through change, and also aided me to find the rest of the tools that I needed to guide me through the next part of my journey.

I think it's also fair to point out that at this stage of my journey I had no real understanding of the fact I was an addict or what that even meant. To me an addict was someone who was dependent on one drug or another. It was to be many many years before I had the exact nature of that problem explained and broken down for me and only then was I ready for the solution. But there was plenty of tears and water under the bridge to come before that day'.

to be continued

Printed in Poland
by Amazon Fulfillment
Poland Sp. z o.o., Wrocław